100
SUPERHEROES & VILLAINS
COLORING BOOK FOR ADULTS
Anxiety & Stress Relief

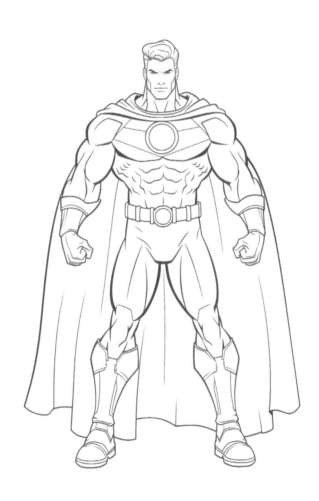

100
SUPERHEROES & VILLAINS
COLORING BOOK FOR ADULTS
Anxiety & Stress Relief

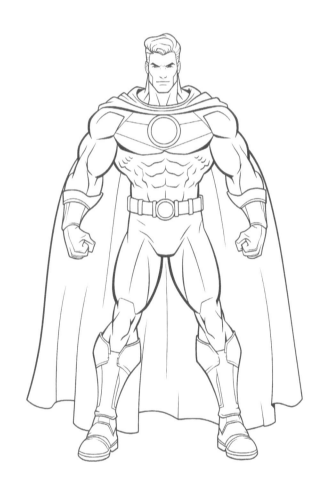

Clara Blake

Copyright © 2023 Clara Blake

All rights reserved. No part of this book may be reproduced or used in any manner without the prior written permission of the copyright owner, except for the use of brief quotations in a book review.

To request permissions, contact the publisher at hello@clarablake.art.

Paperback: 979-8-89172-117-3
Hardcover: 979-8-89172-118-0

First paperback edition September 2023.

Edited by Clara Blake
Cover by Gabriel Cavalheiro
Layout by Gabriel Cavalheiro
Illustrations by Clara Blake

"The creative adult is the child who survived."

— *Ursula K. Le Guin (1929 - 2018)*

With love to my kids,
the most creative people
I've ever known.

Dear Colorist,

I hope you're enjoying your creative journey through this coloring book as much as we enjoyed creating it for you. Your feedback means the world to us!

If you've had a positive experience with **"100 Superheroes & Villains**," we kindly invite you to share your thoughts on Amazon with a star rating and a few words about your coloring adventure.

Your honest review will brighten our day and help fellow coloring enthusiasts discover the joy this book brings. Thank you for being a part of our coloring community, and happy coloring!

With colorful wishes,

Clara Blake

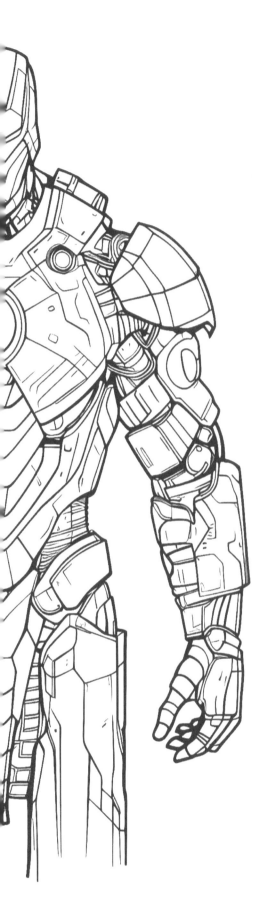

FOREWORD

*W*elcome to the world of Superheroes & Villains!

This coloring book is designed to transport you into the thrilling universe of superheroes and villains. Within these pages, you'll find a dynamic array of captivating designs, each eagerly awaiting your artistic touch to unleash their heroic or villainous essence.

Coloring offers a meditative escape from our busy lives, a simple joy often forgotten in adulthood. "100 Superheroes & Villains" revives this therapeutic magic, inviting artists of all levels to reconnect with their inner child and set their imagination free.

Superheroes and villains, celebrated for their extraordinary powers and timeless appeal, have ignited human imaginations for generations. This book pays tribute to their diverse personas, from the valiant superheroes of comic books to the cunning villains of cinematic lore. Each character invites you to immerse yourself in their world, explore their essence, and infuse your artistic expression with a palette of vibrant colors.

Here are some tips for coloring this book:

- Start by choosing a pattern that you find appealing. There is no right or wrong answer, so just go with your gut.
- Once you have chosen a pattern, take some time to study it. Look at the different shapes and colors, and think about how you want to color them.
- Don't be afraid to experiment with different colors and techniques. Use a variety of colors to create a more interesting effect and add some shading to create depth and dimension. You can even use a white gel pen to add highlights. There is no right or wrong way to color, so just have fun and see what you come up with.
- If you get stuck, take a break and come back to it later. Sometimes, the best way to solve a problem is to take a step back and clear your head.

As you dive into the thrilling world of superheroes and villains within these pages, may you uncover a renewed sense of wonder and a deep appreciation for the captivating heroics and complexities of these extraordinary characters.

Happy coloring, and may your journey with "100 Superheroes & Villains" be a truly colorful one!

Clara Blake

COLOR TEST PAGE
Use this page to test colors before applying them to the final pages

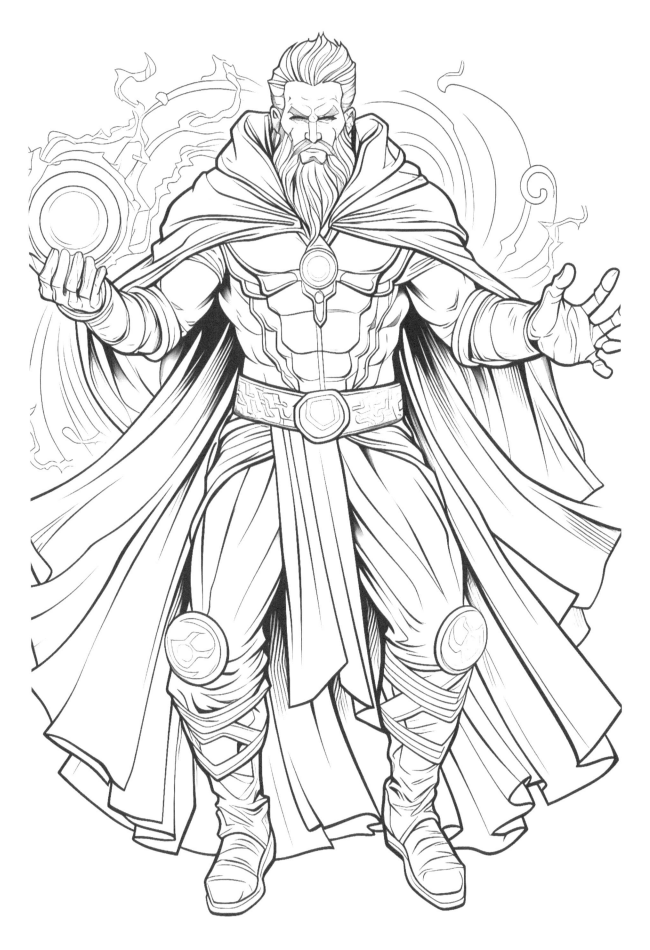

100 SUPERHEROES & VILLAINS *by* CLARA BLAKE

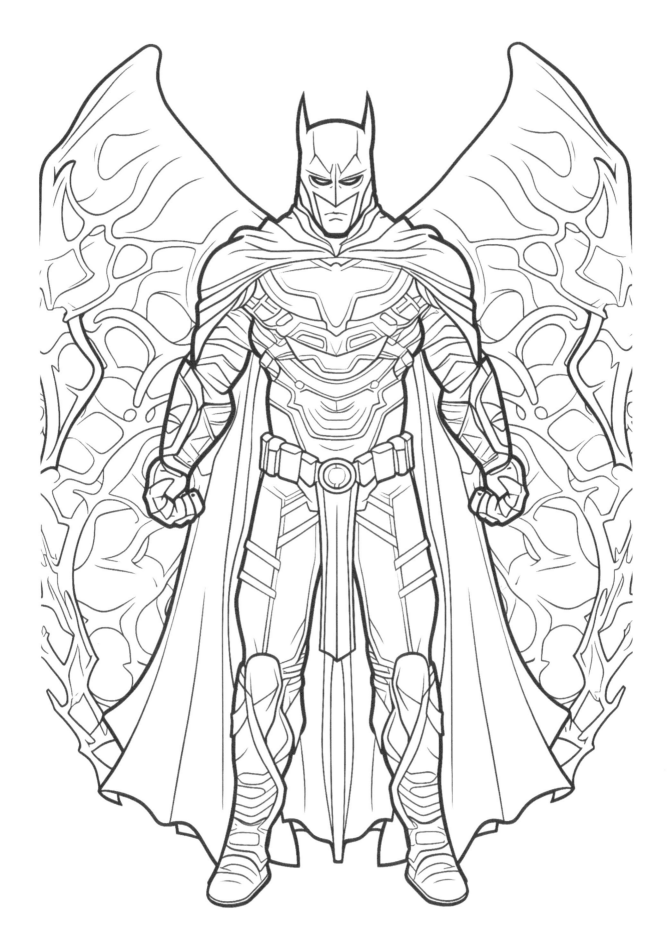

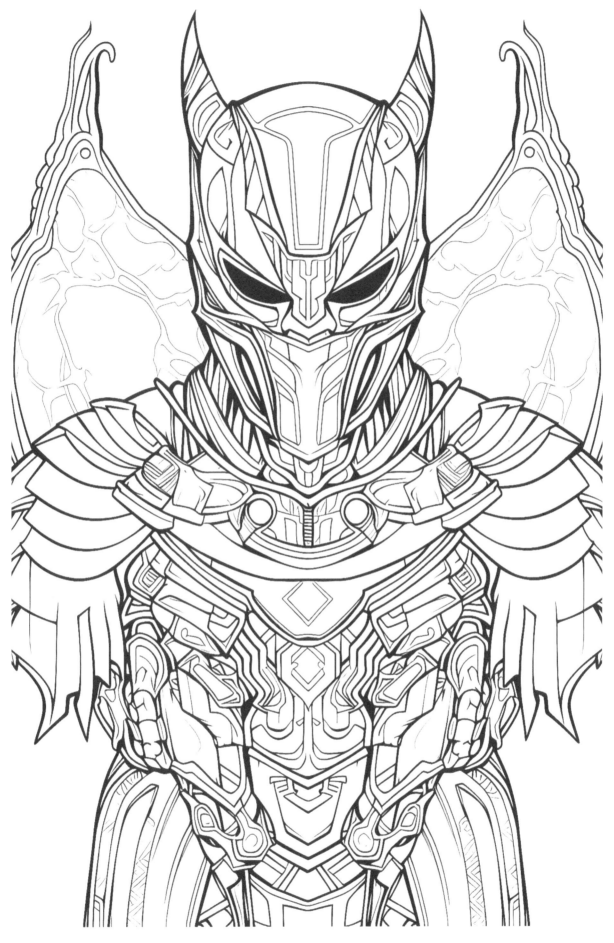

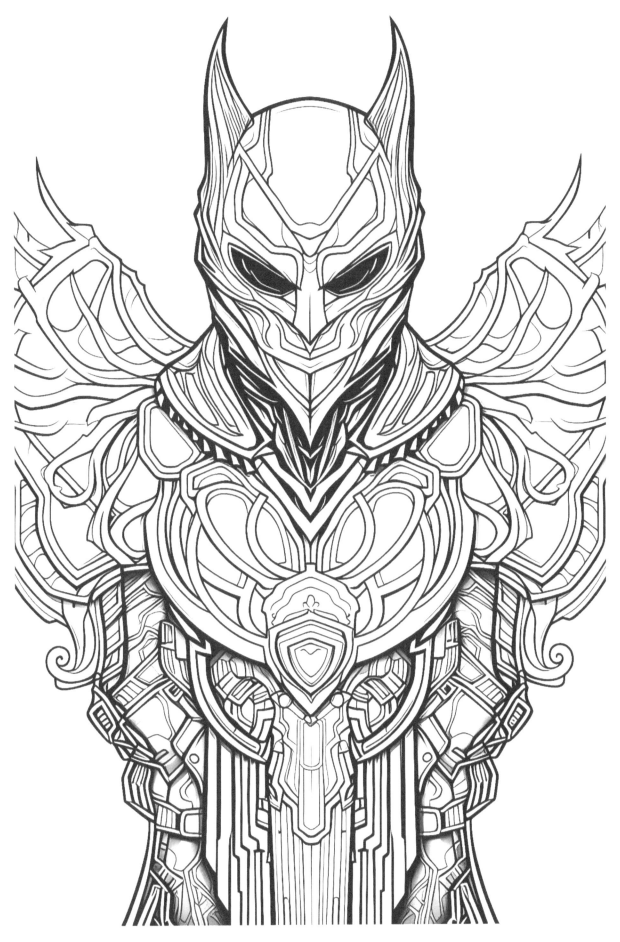

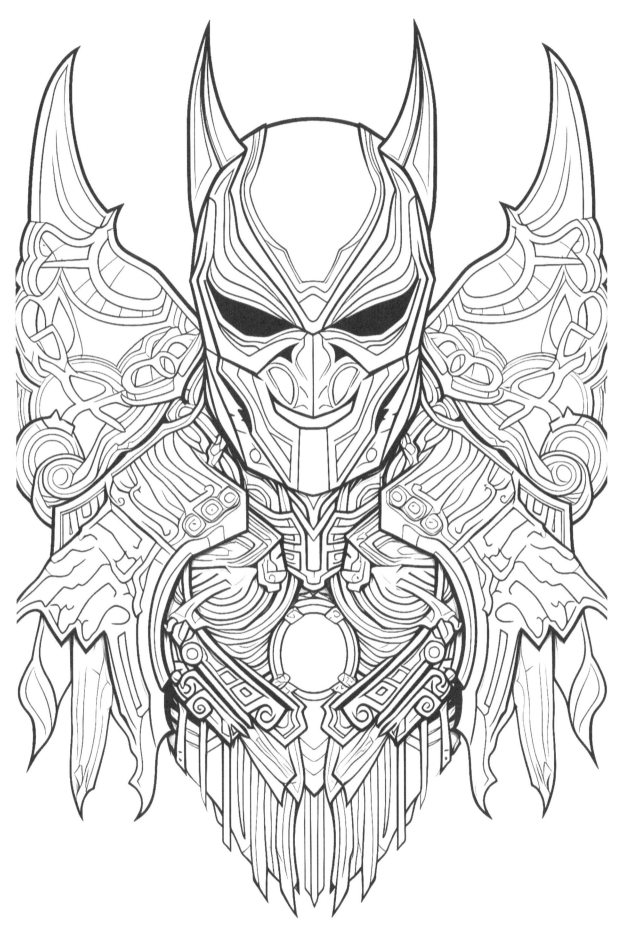

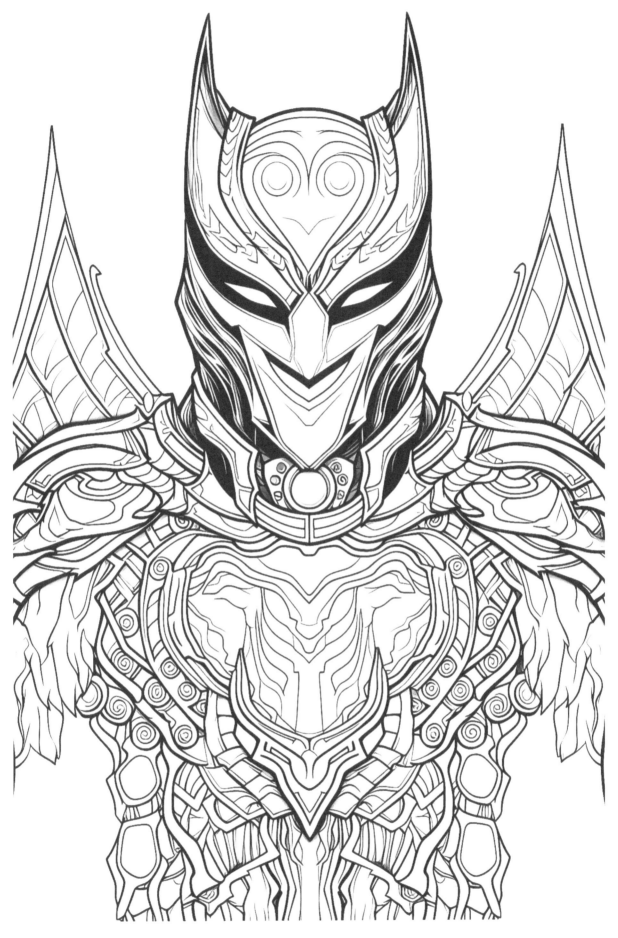

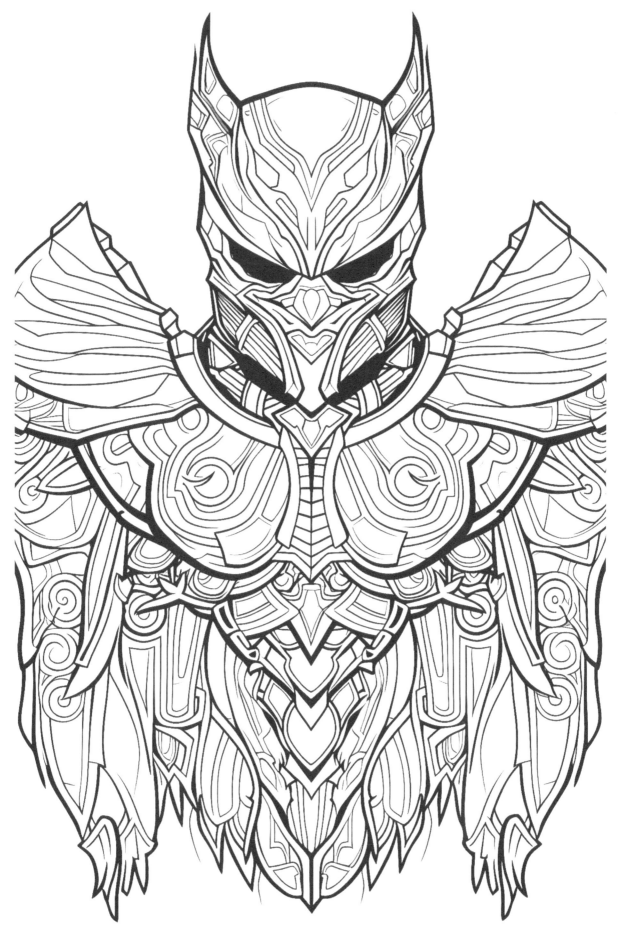

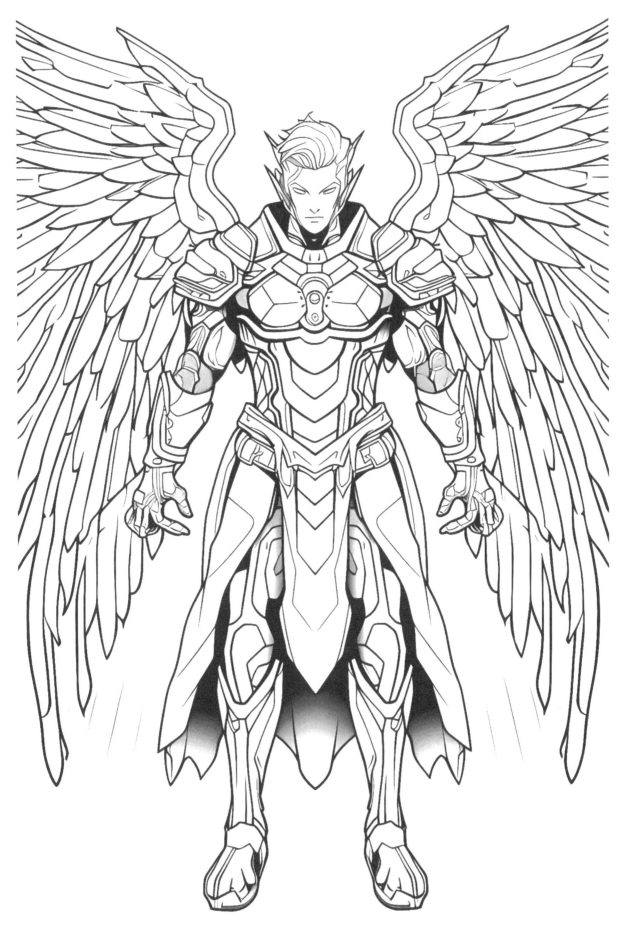

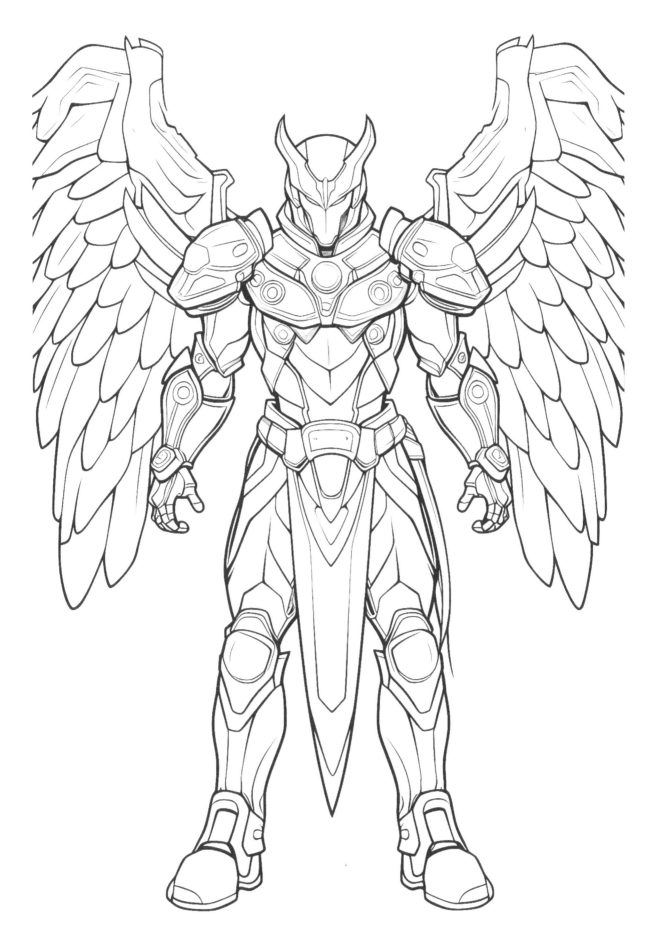

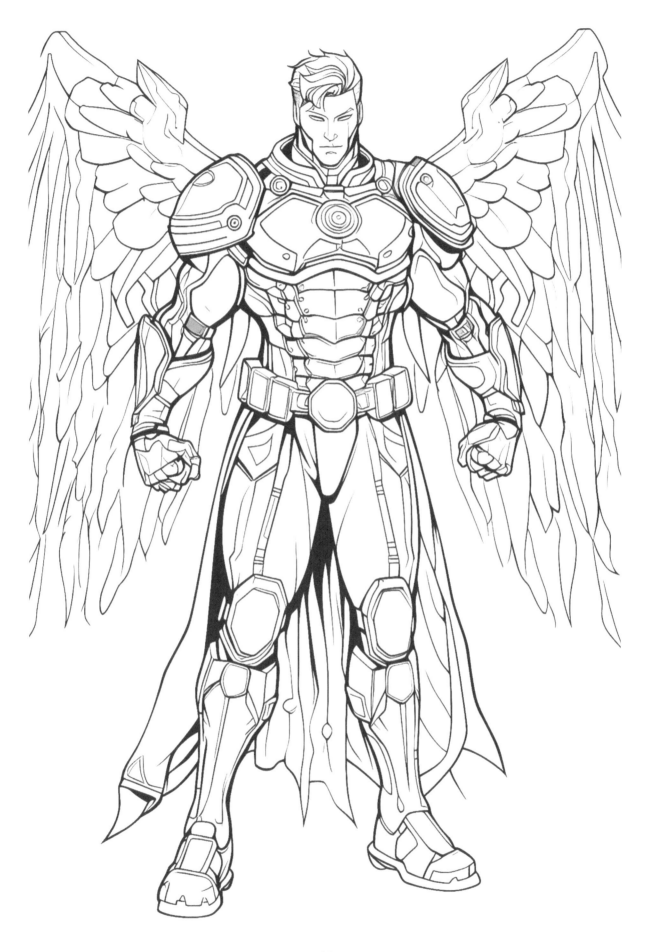

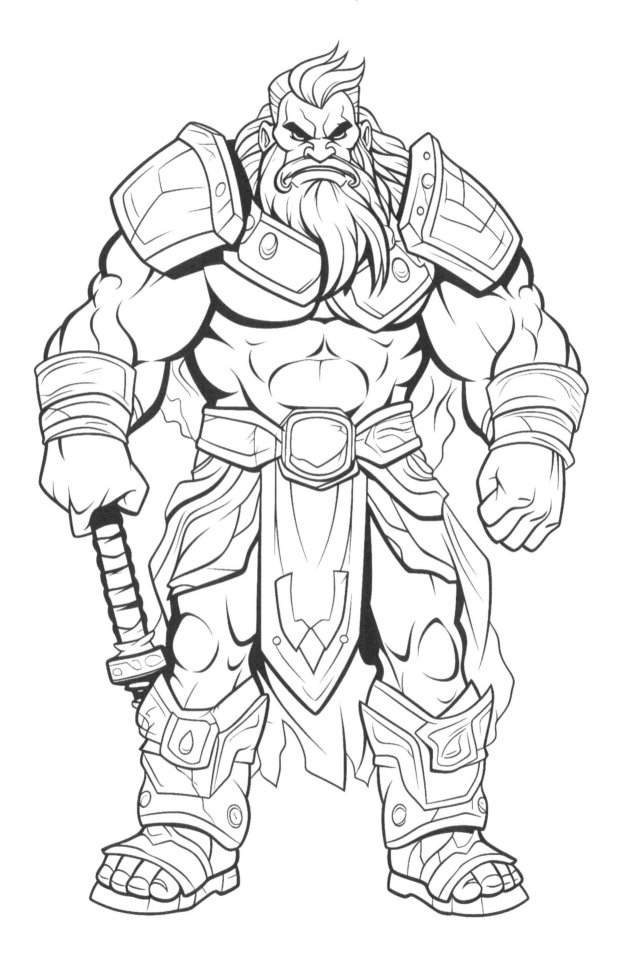

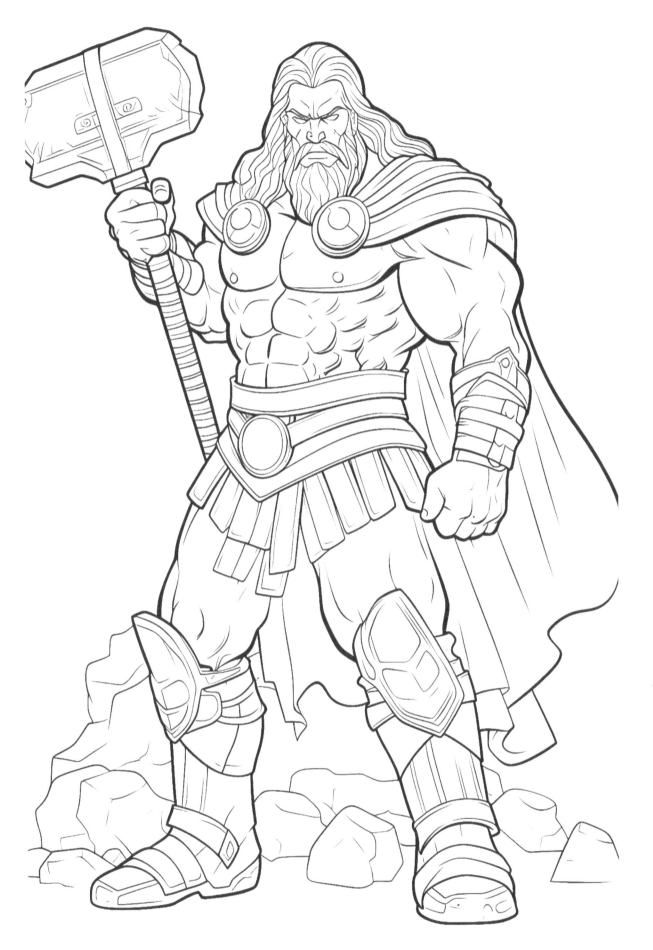

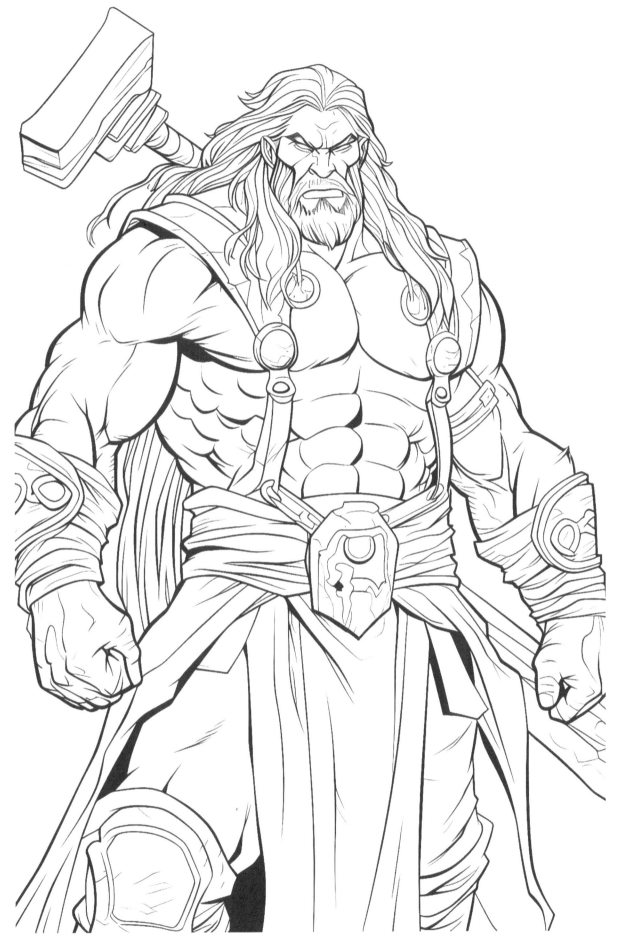

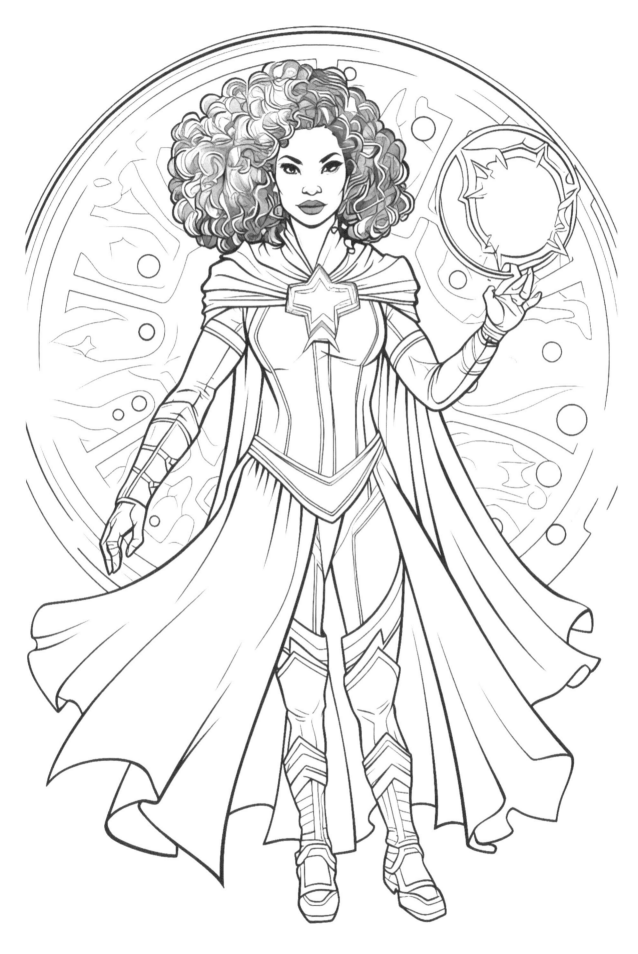

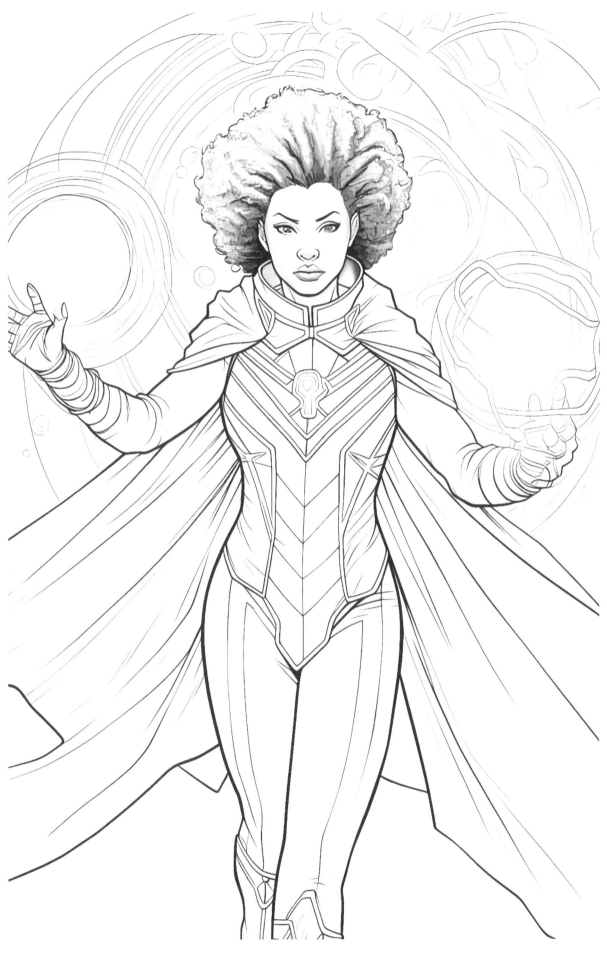

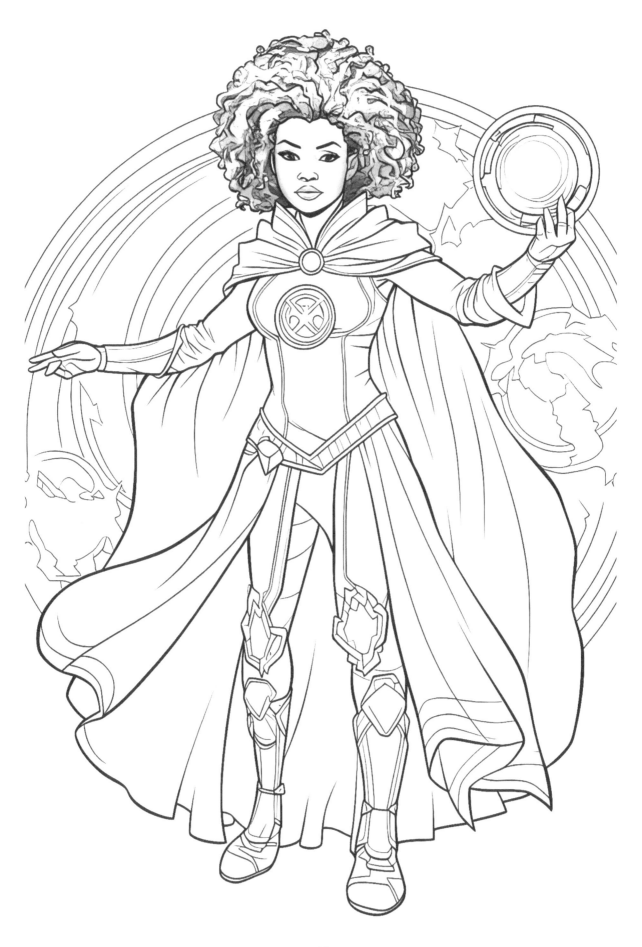

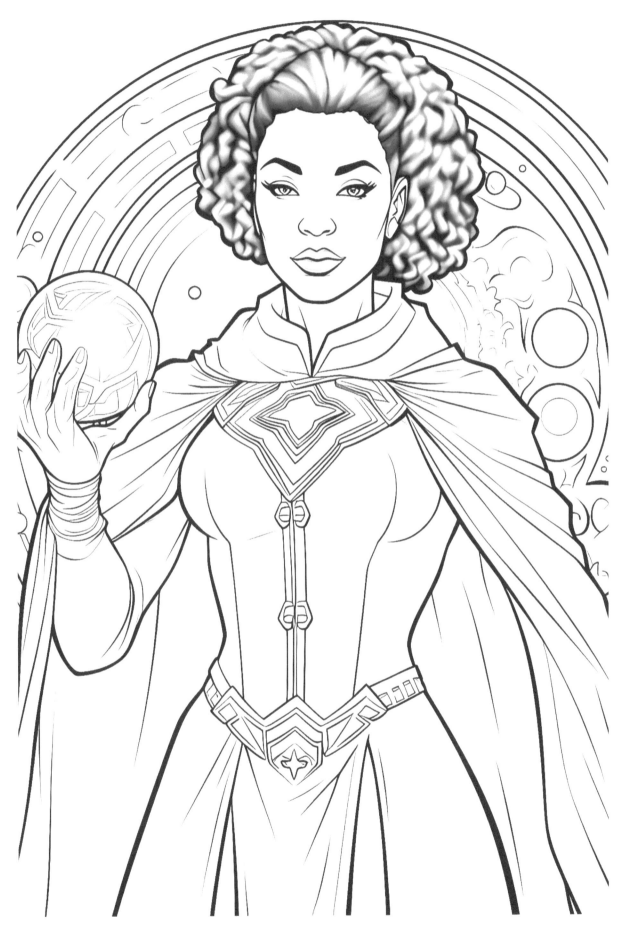

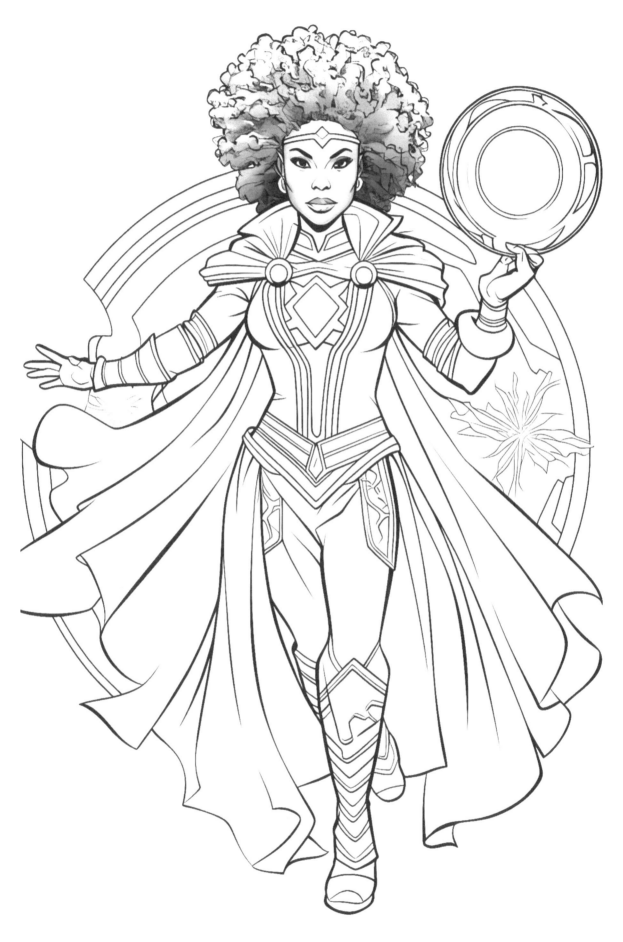

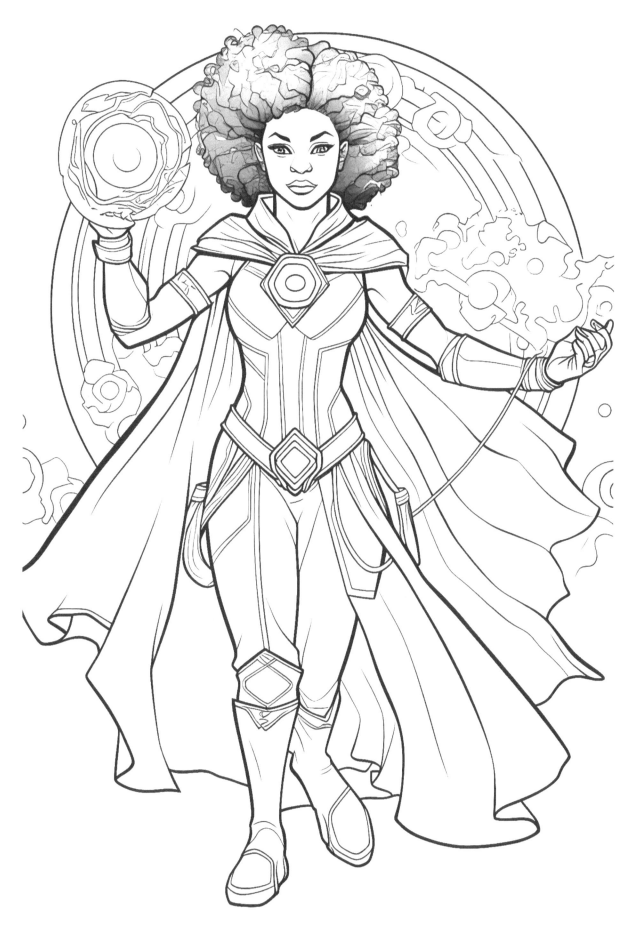

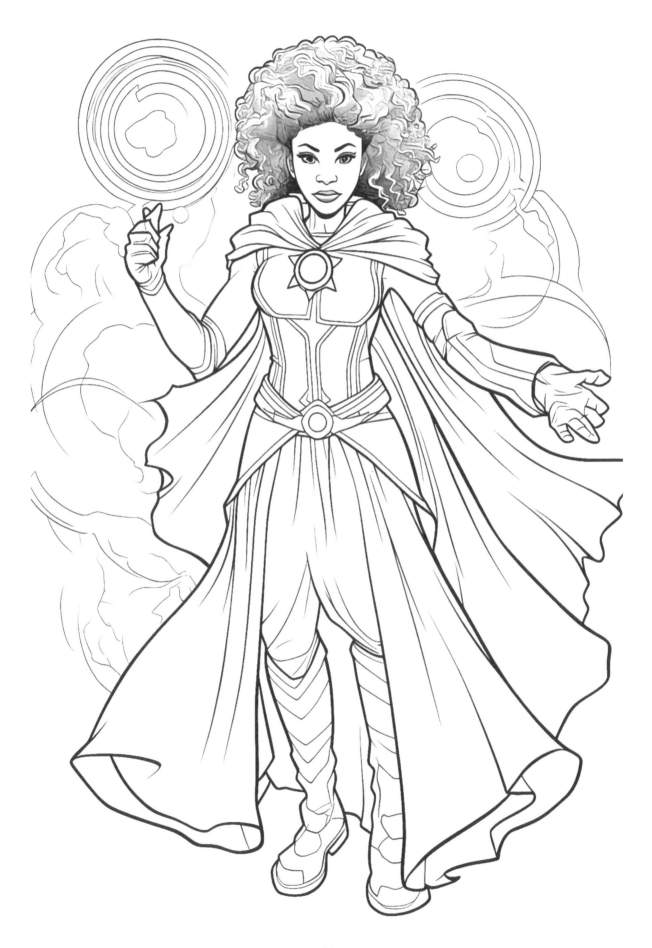

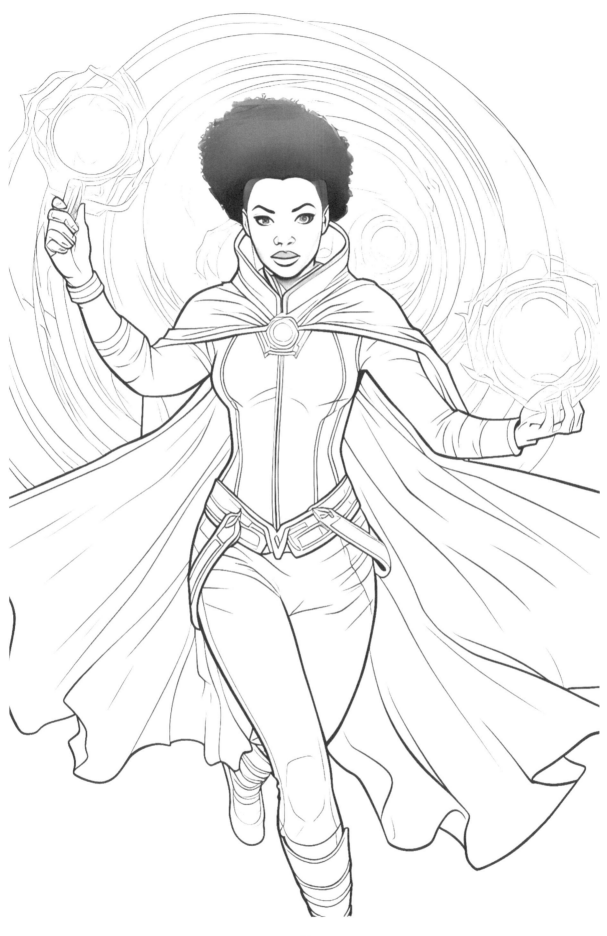

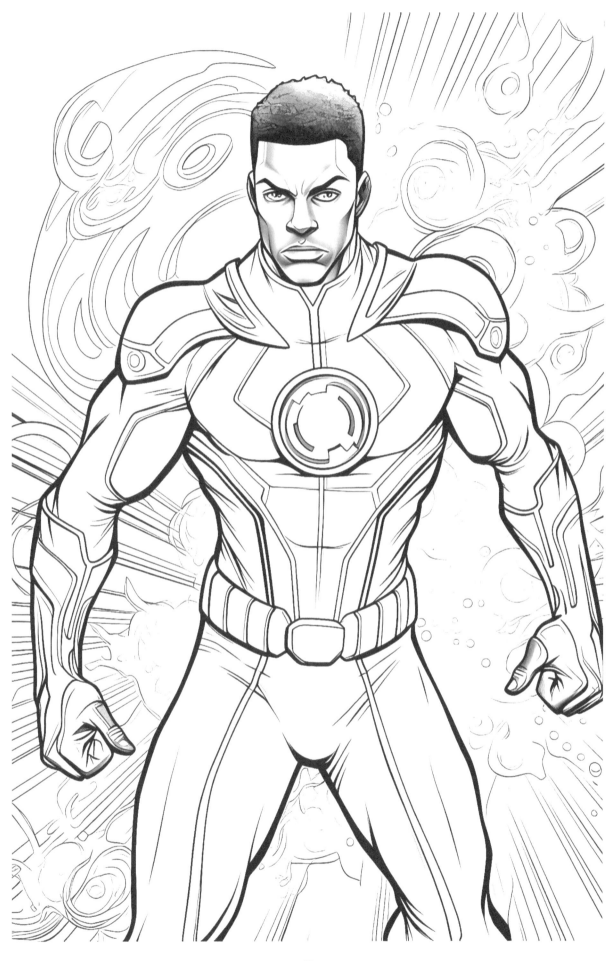

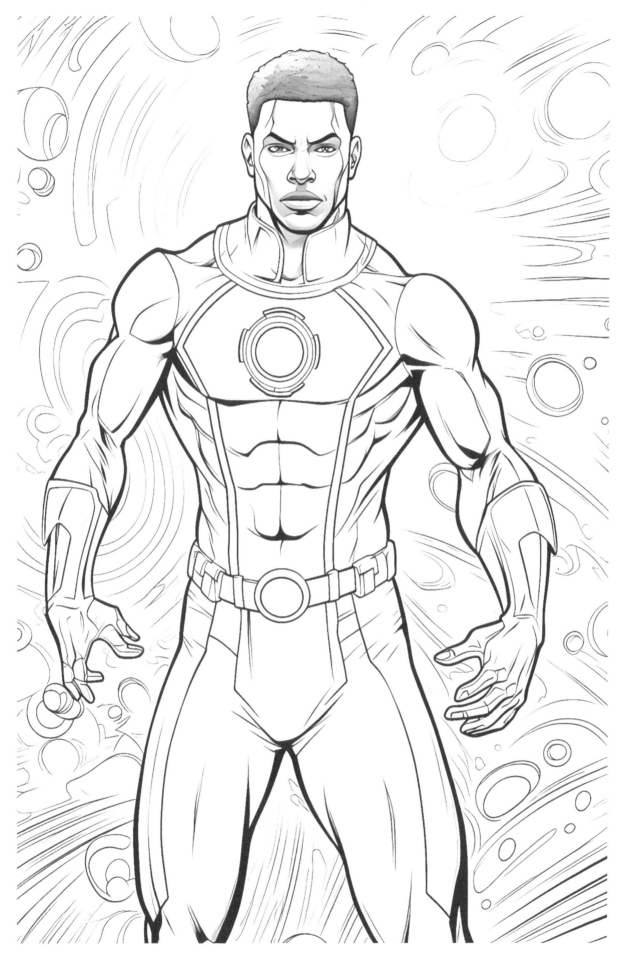

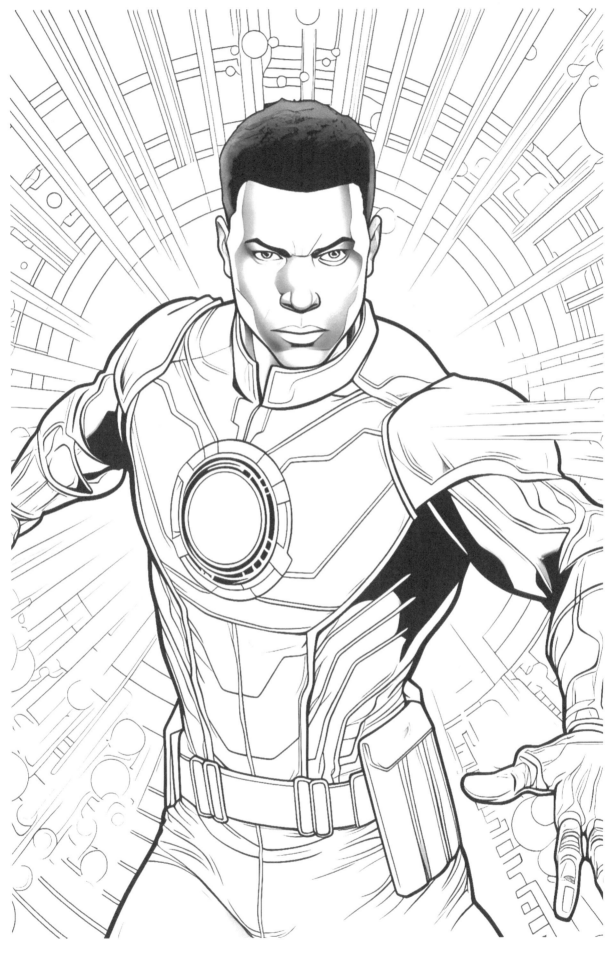

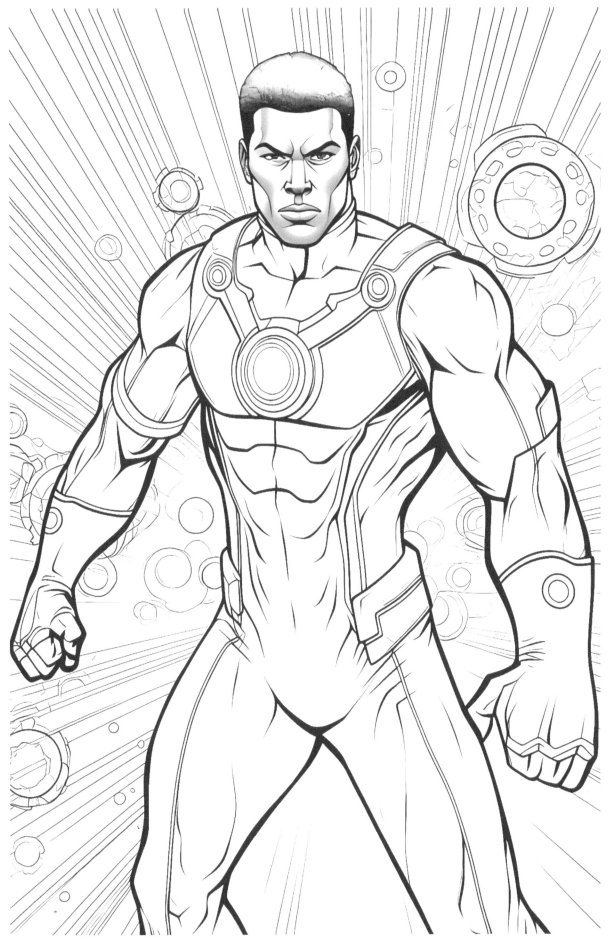

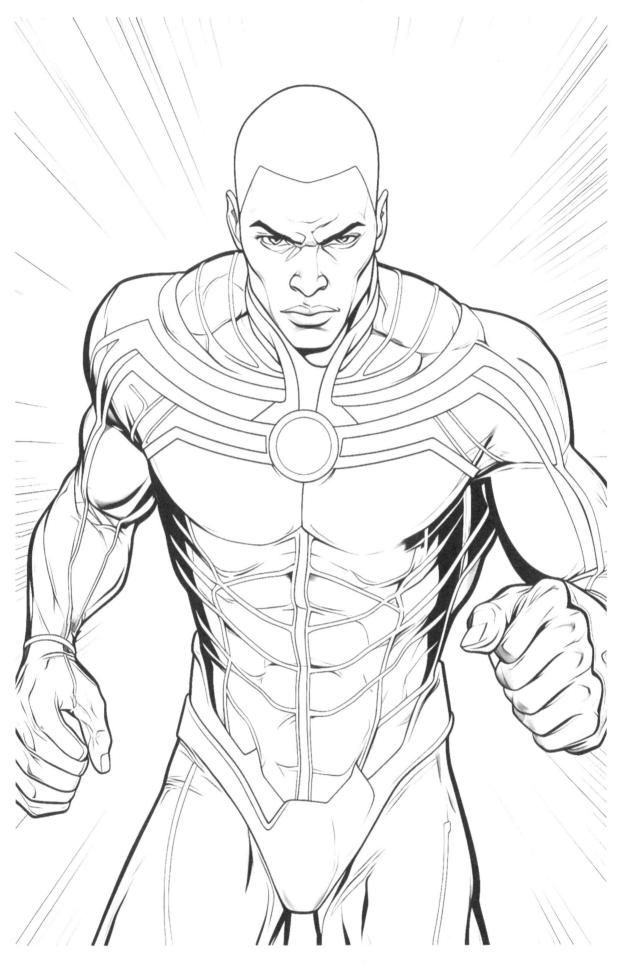

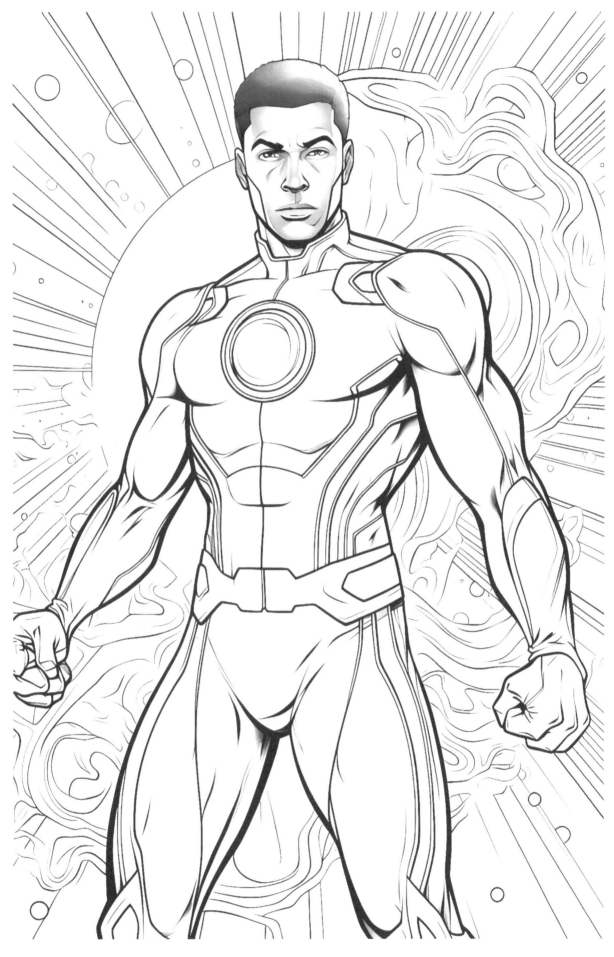

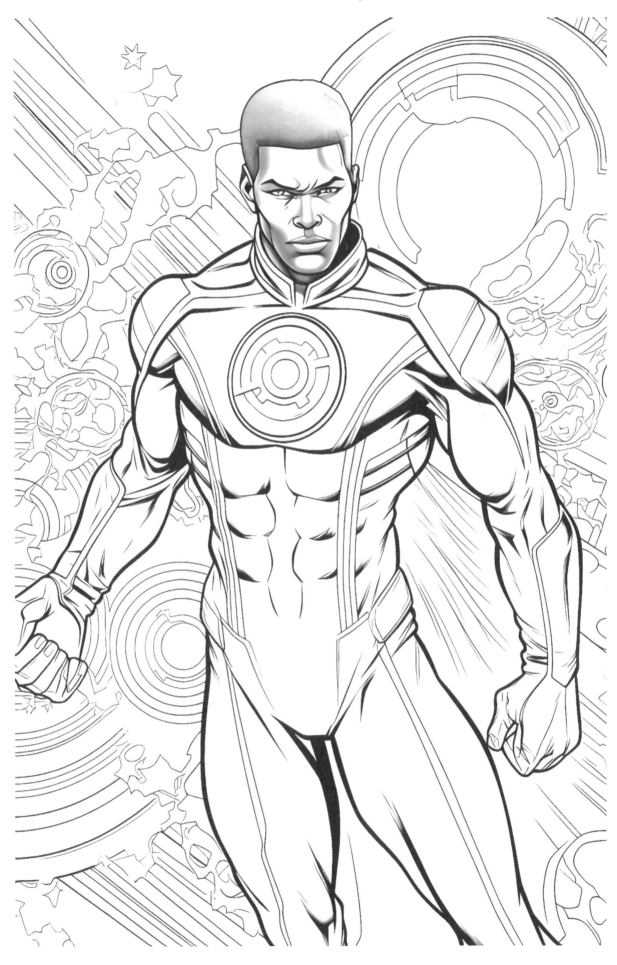

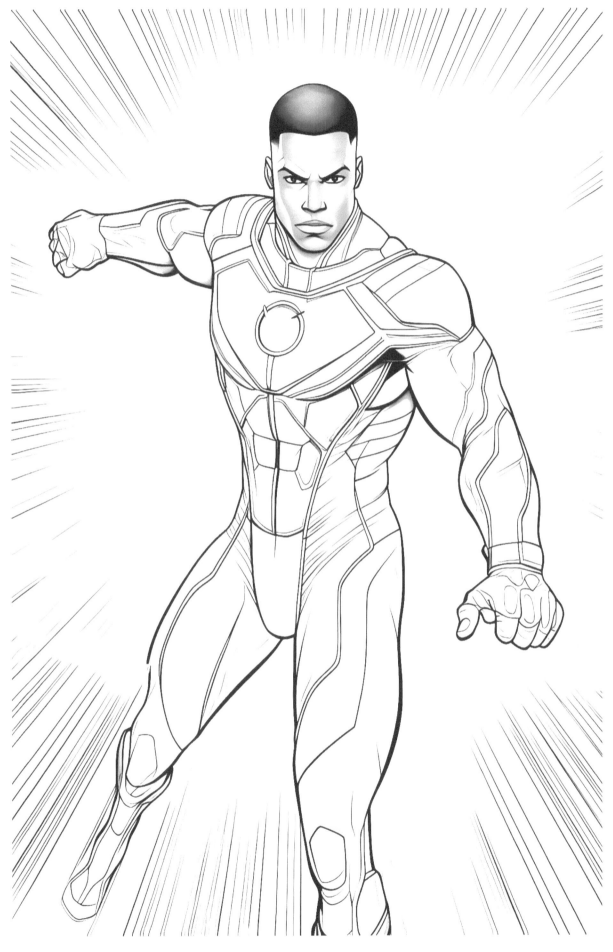

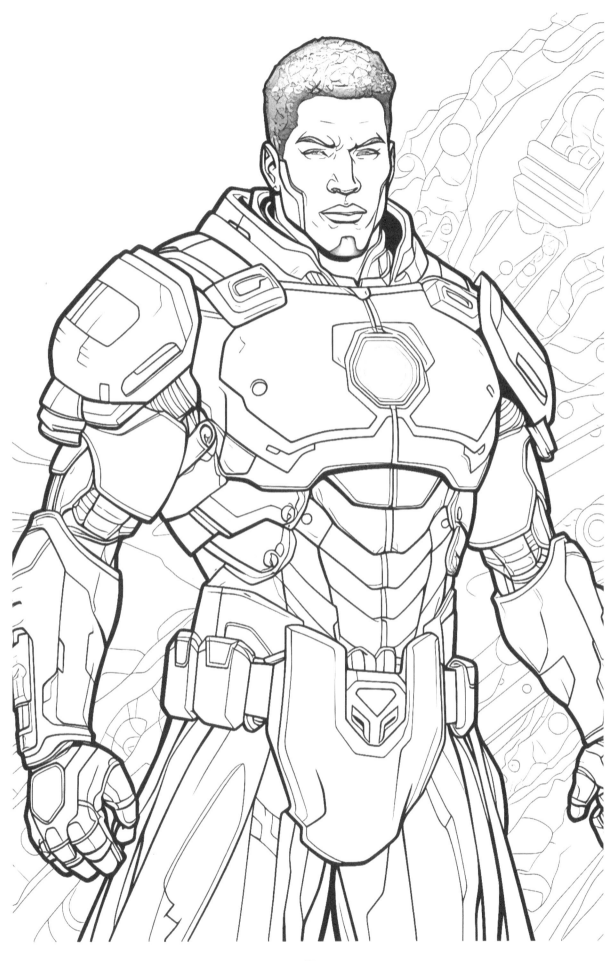

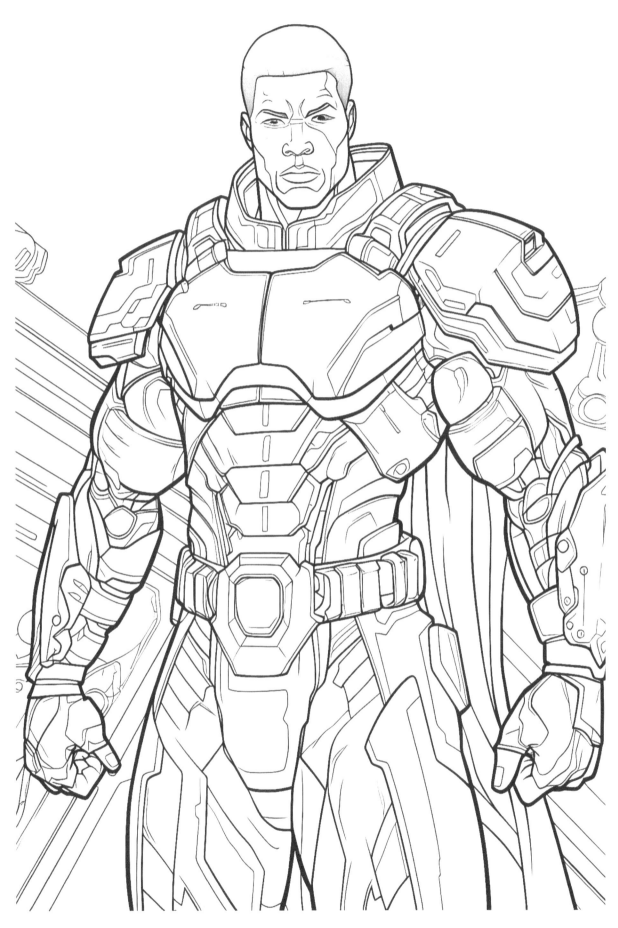

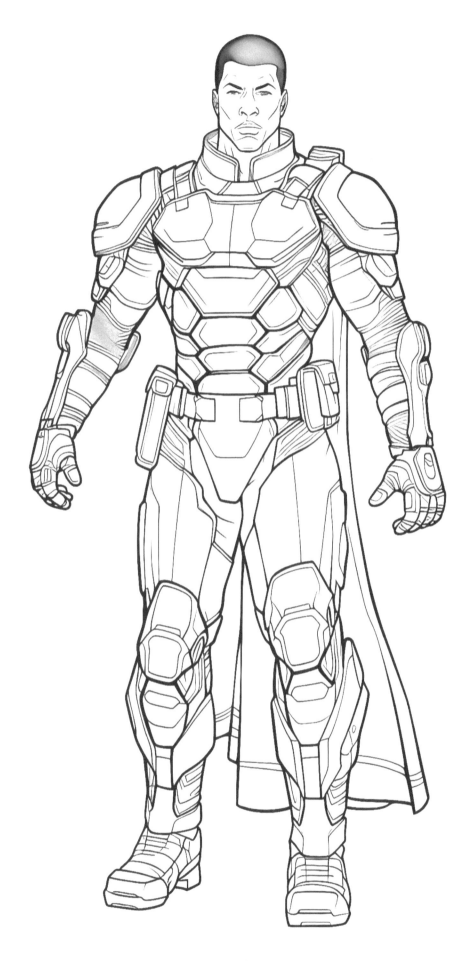

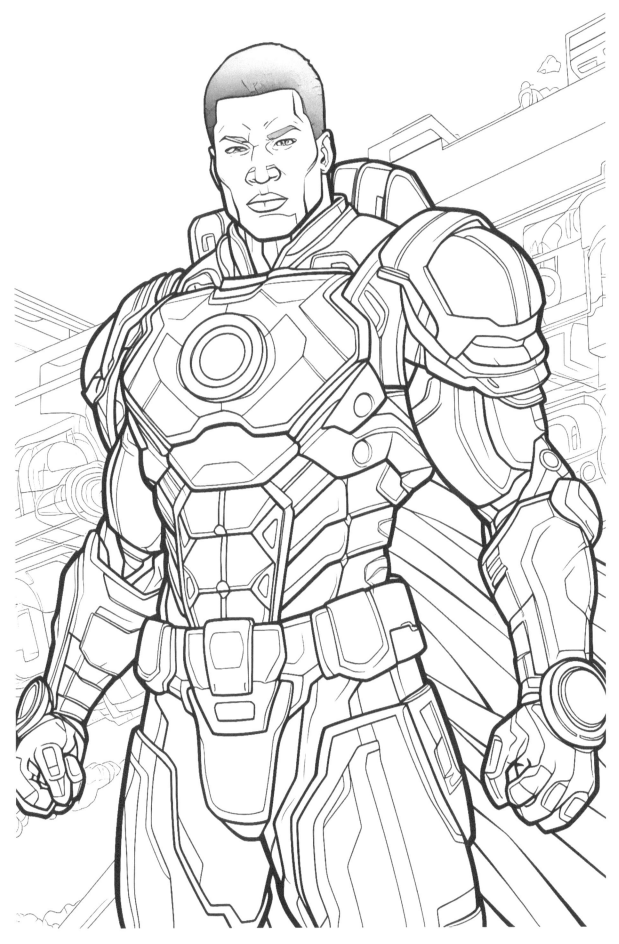

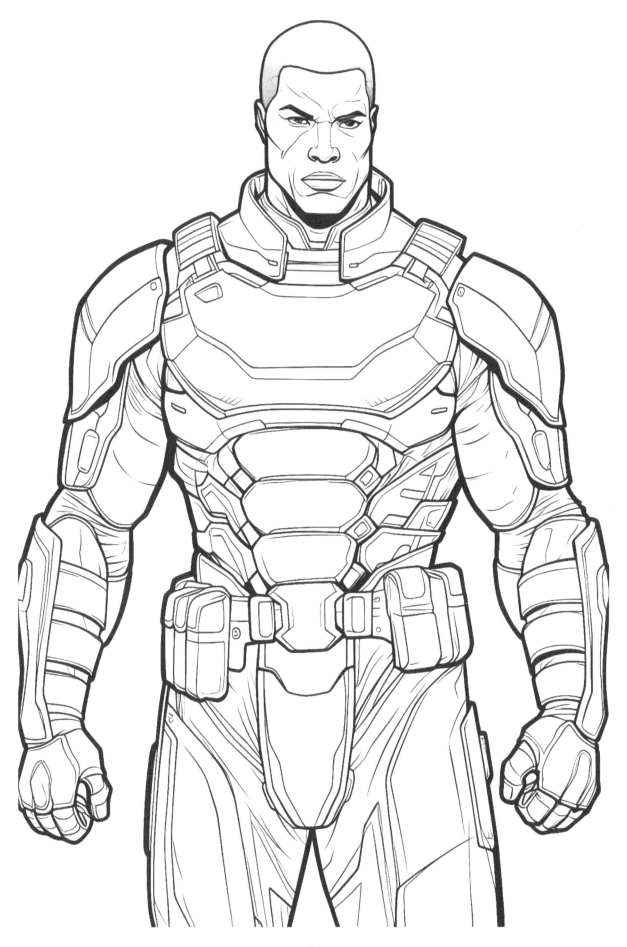

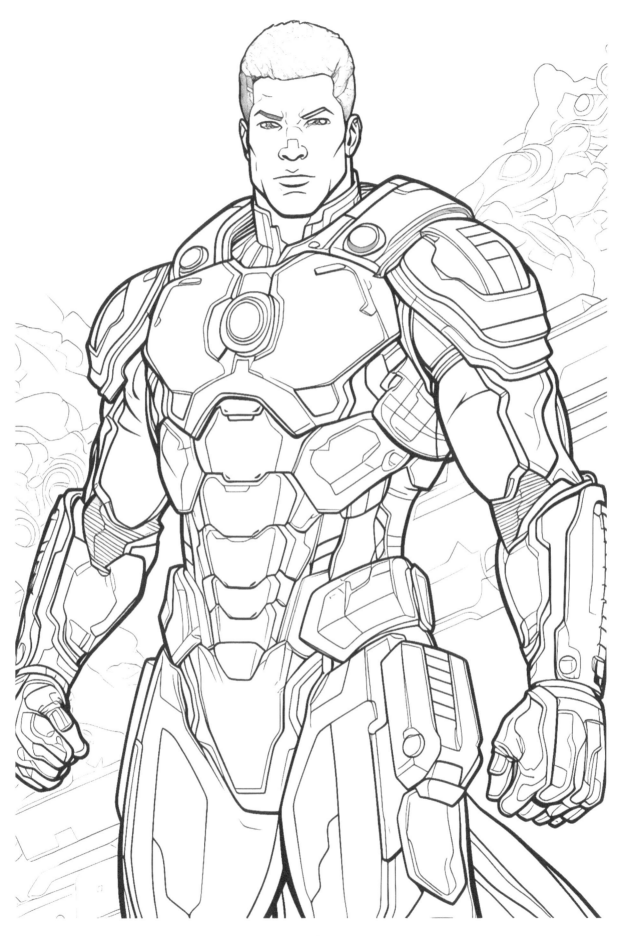

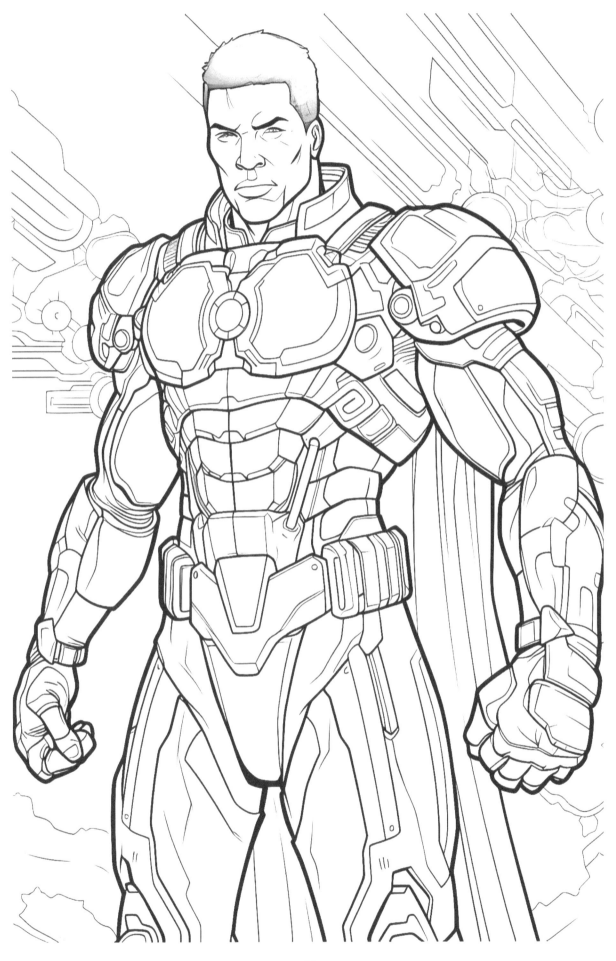

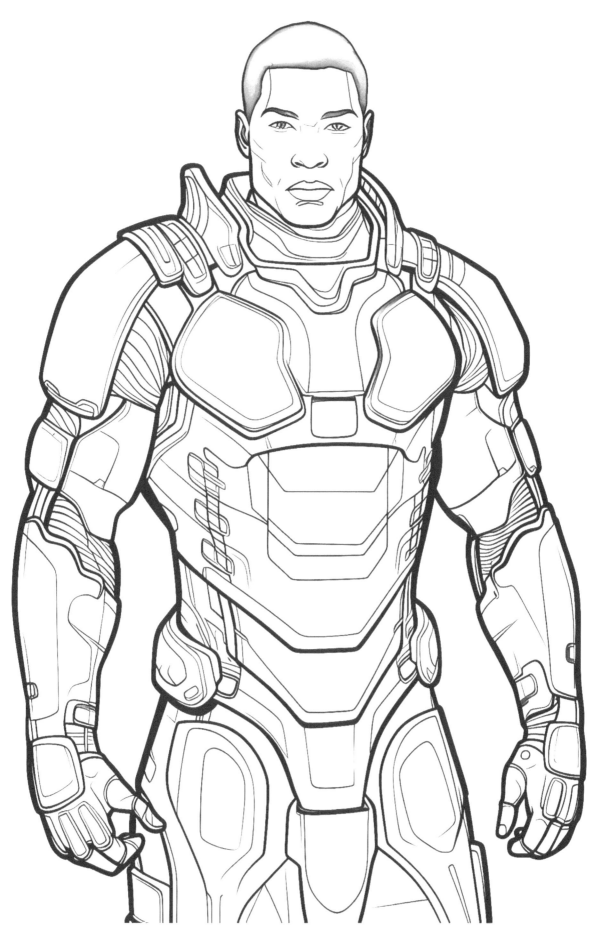

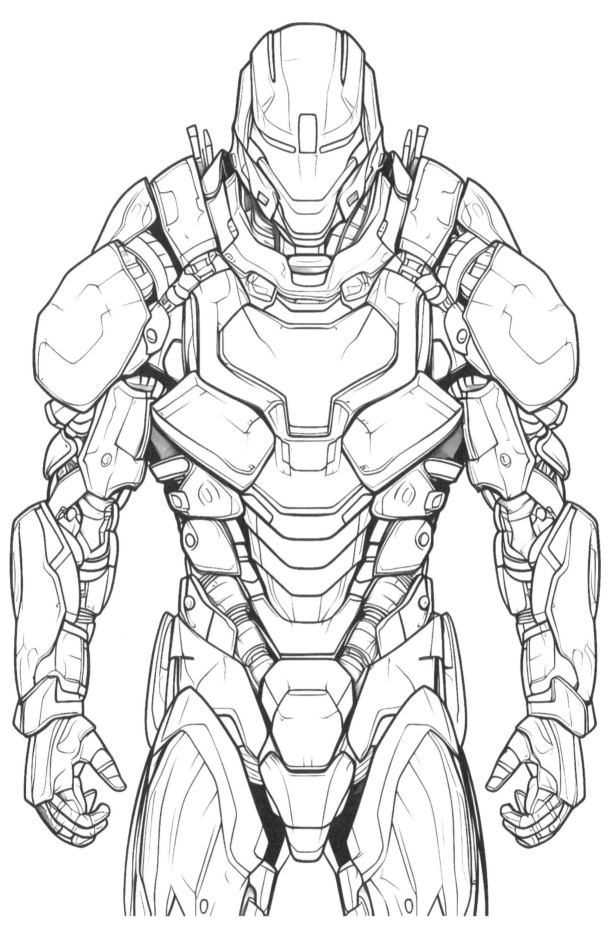

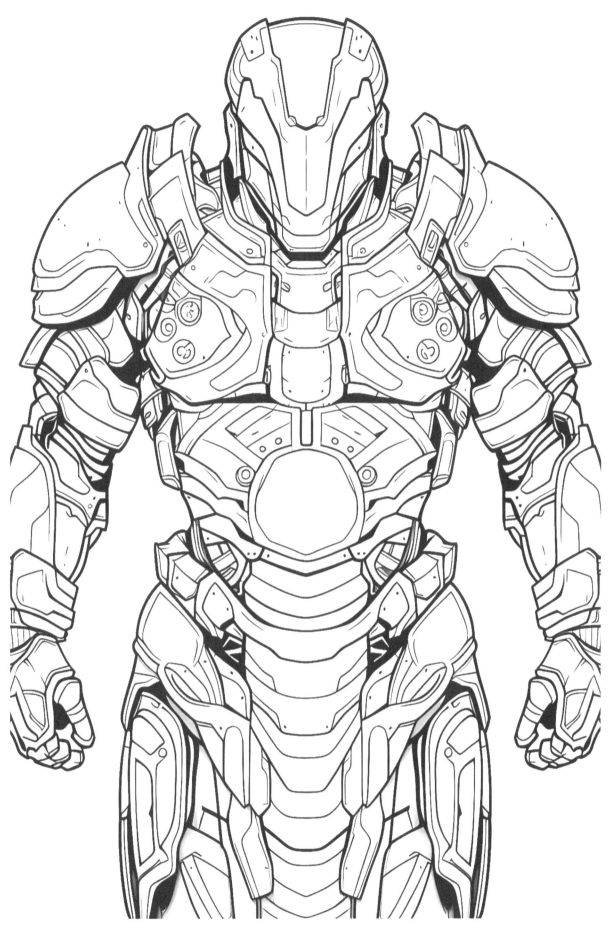

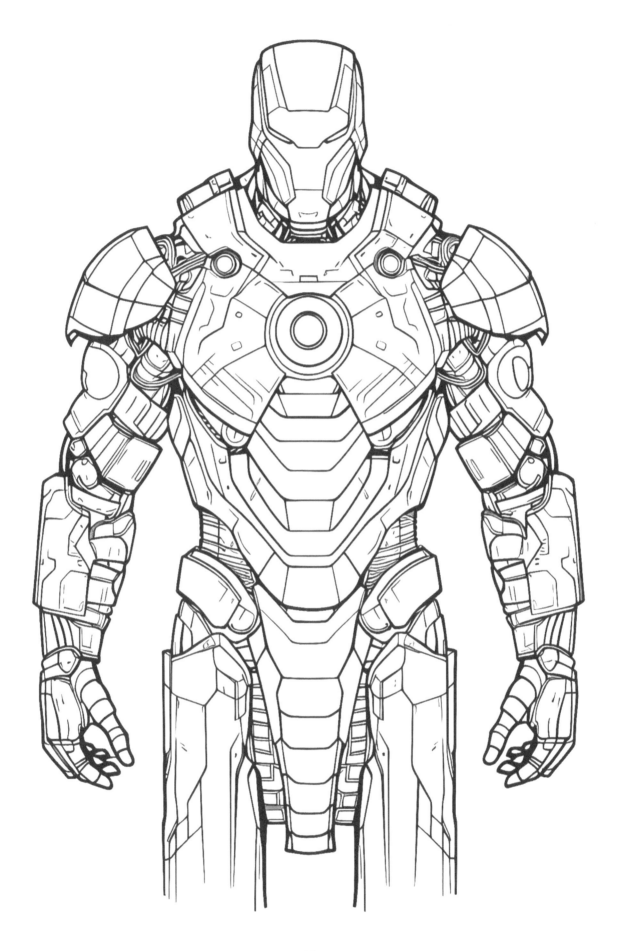

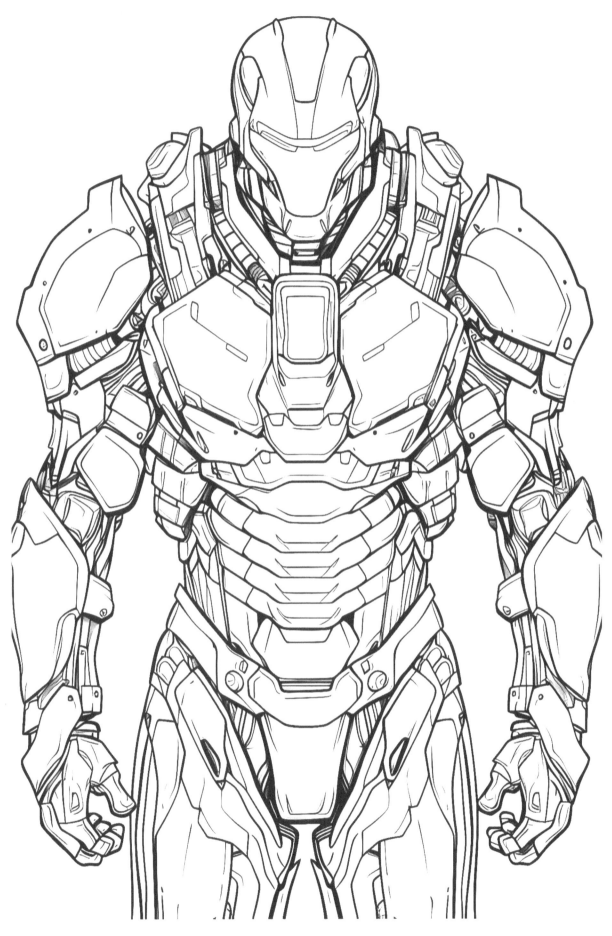

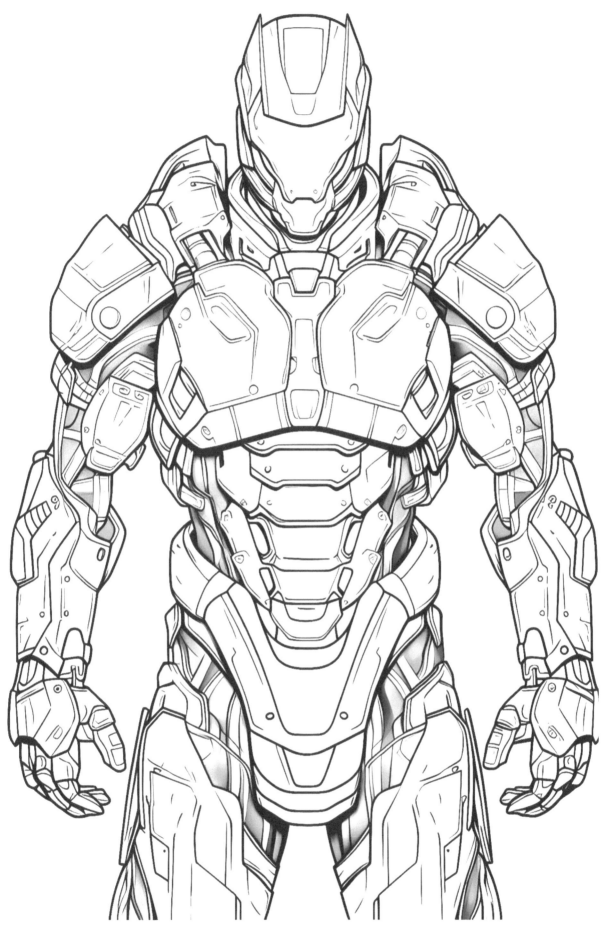

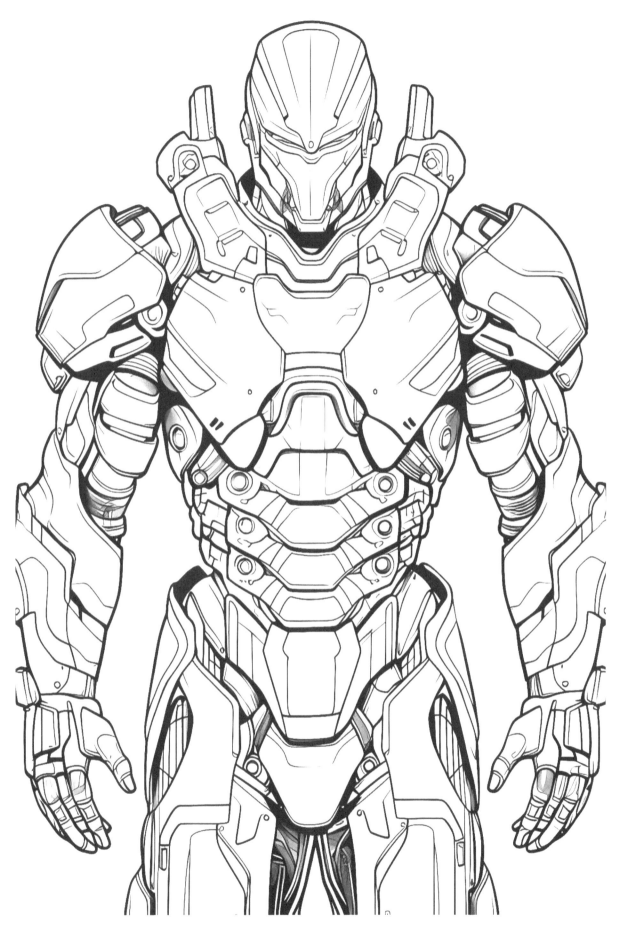

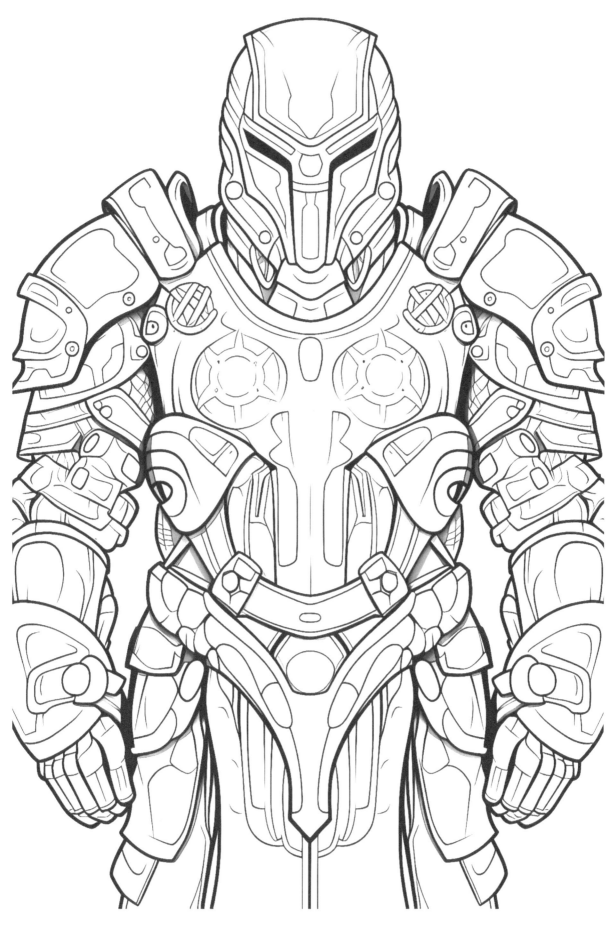

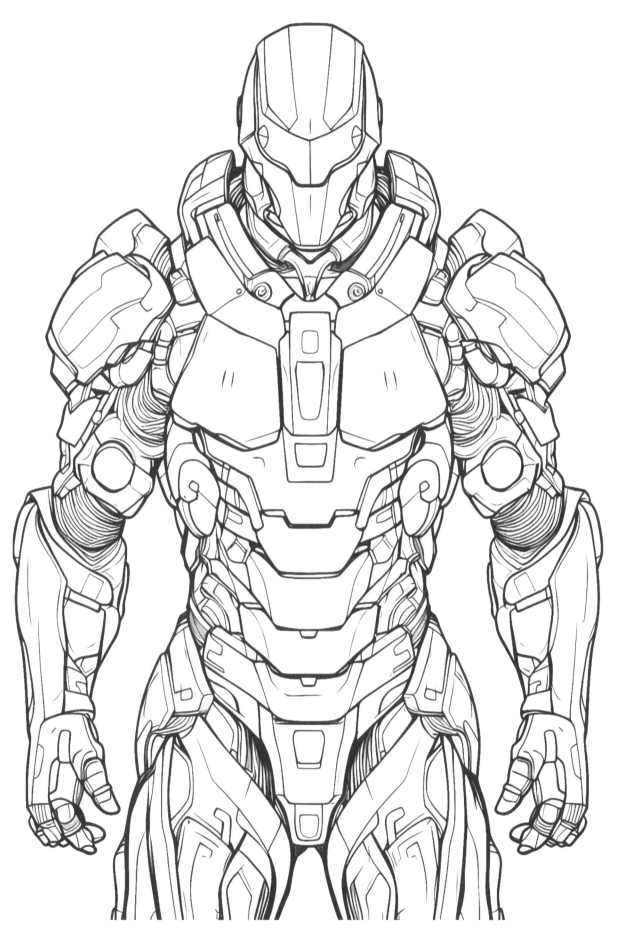

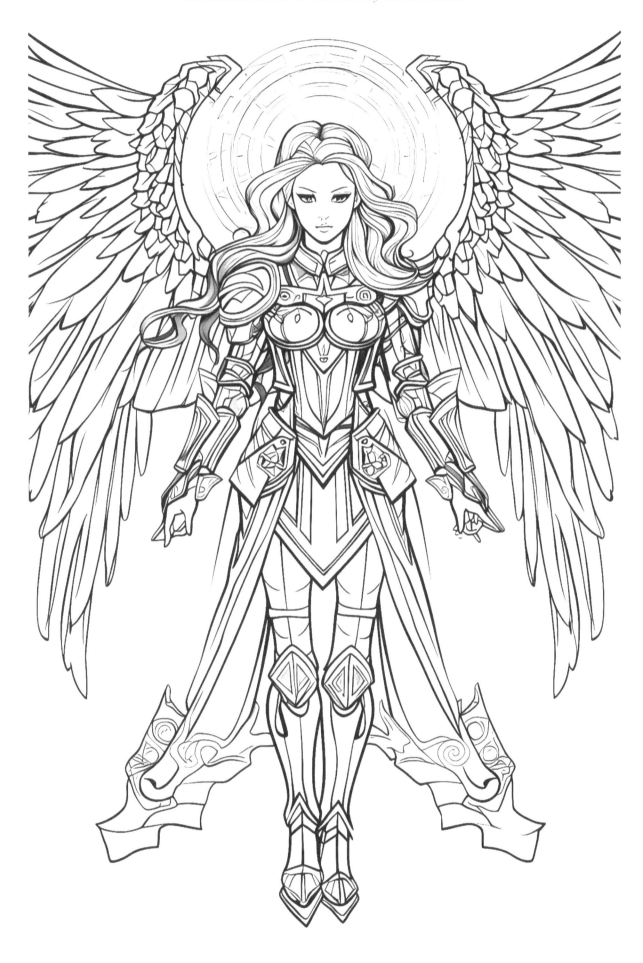

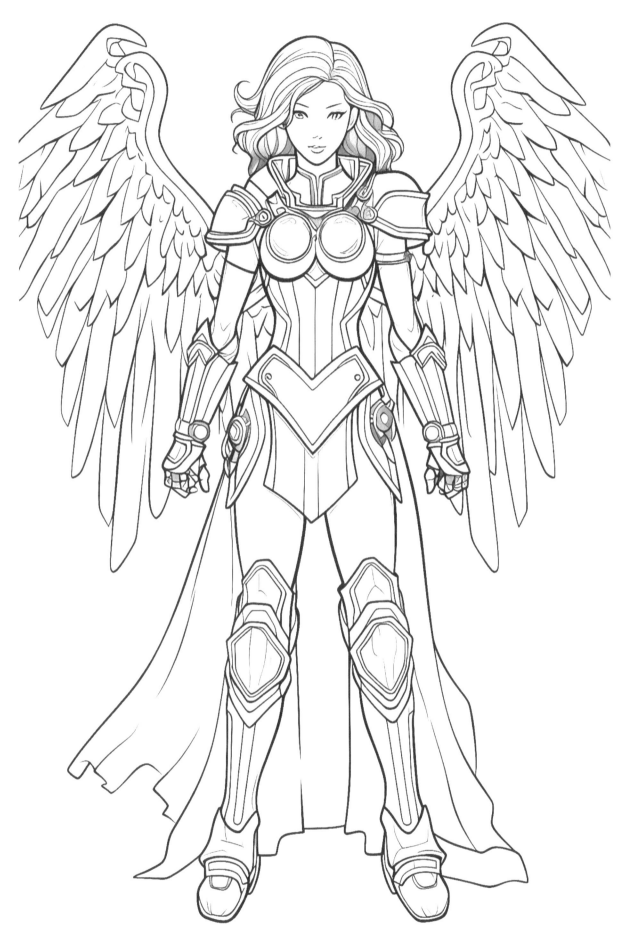

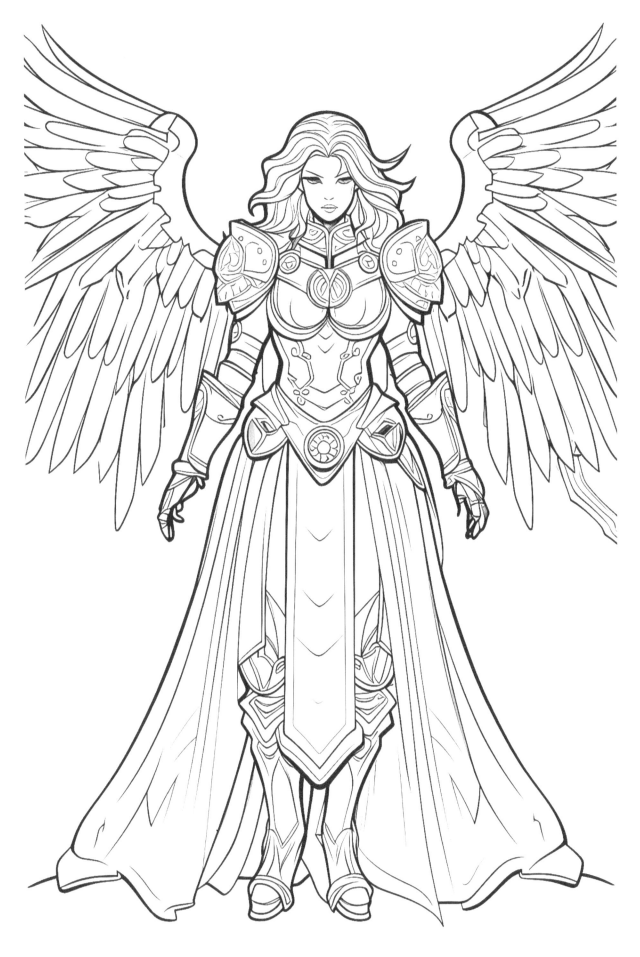

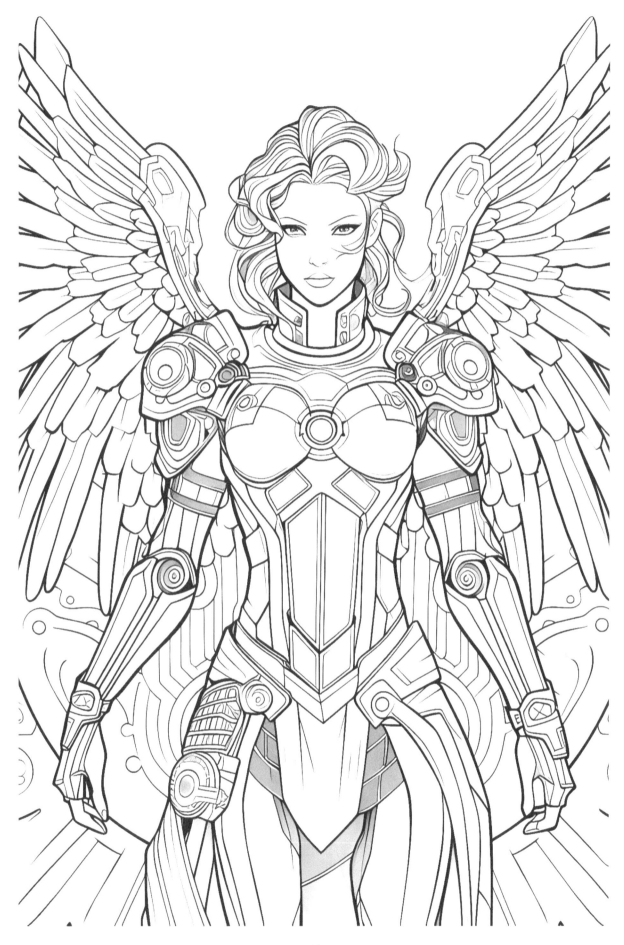

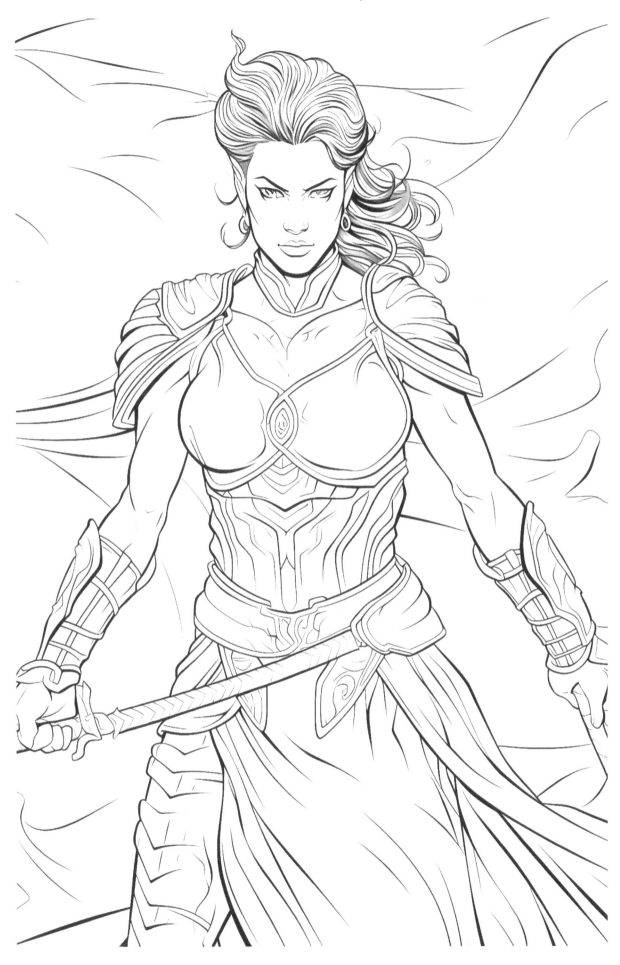

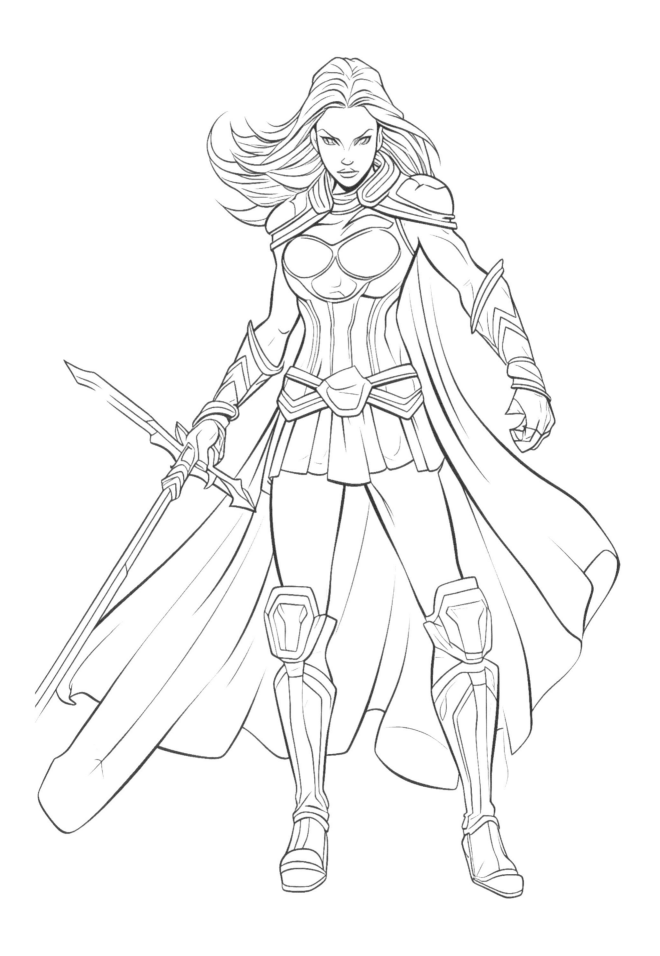

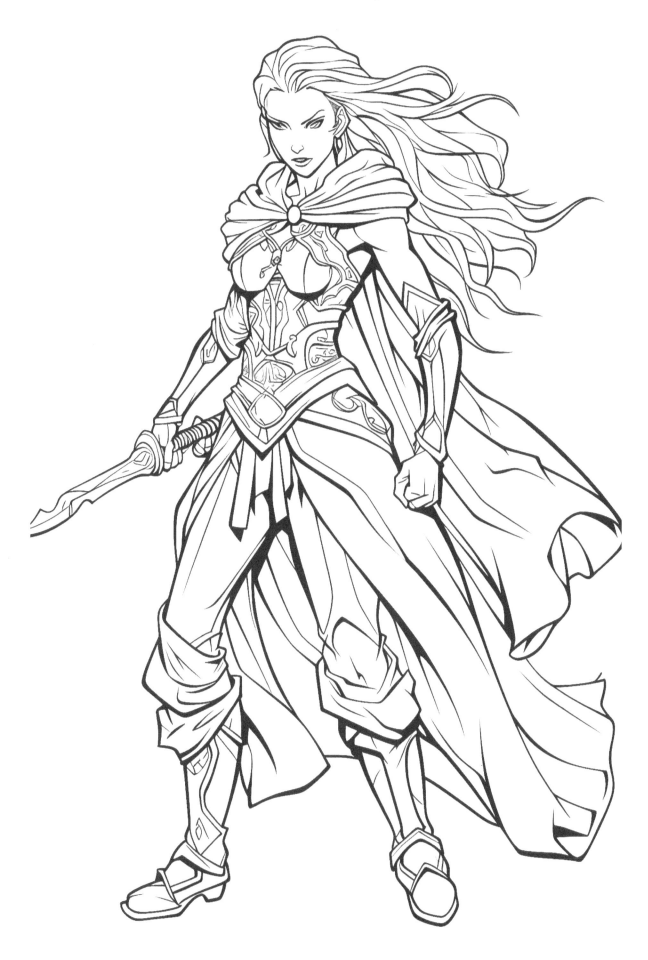

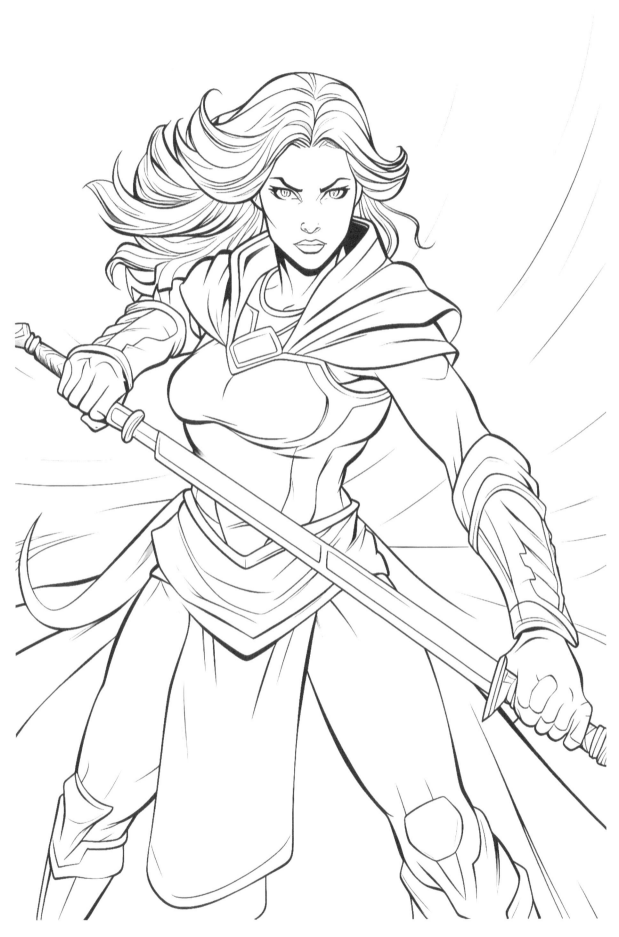

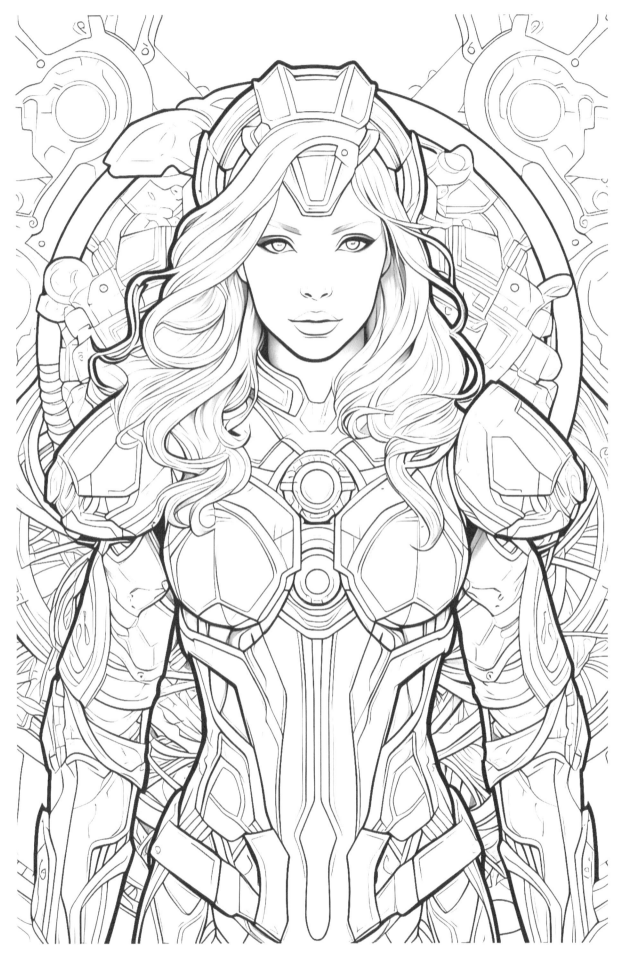

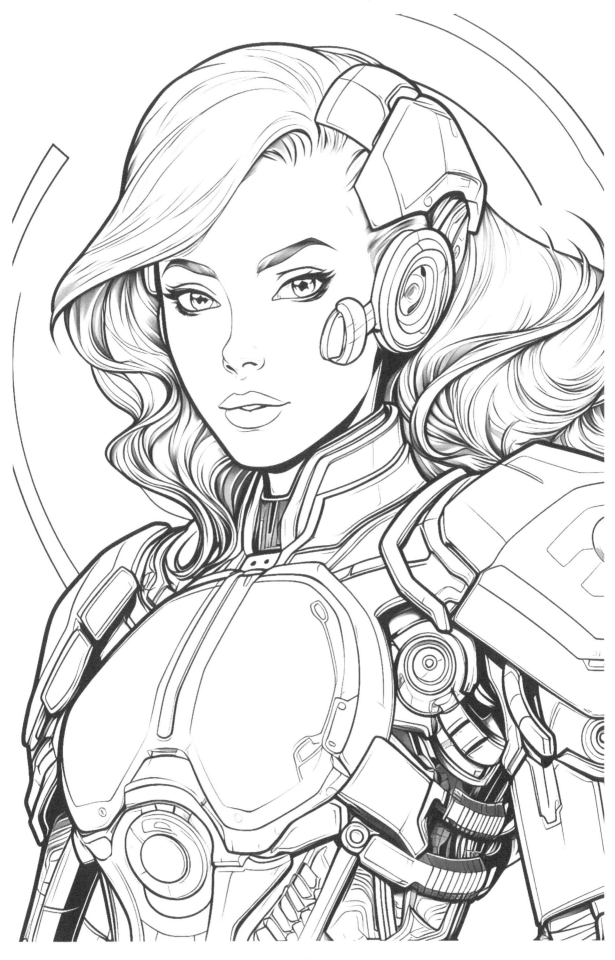

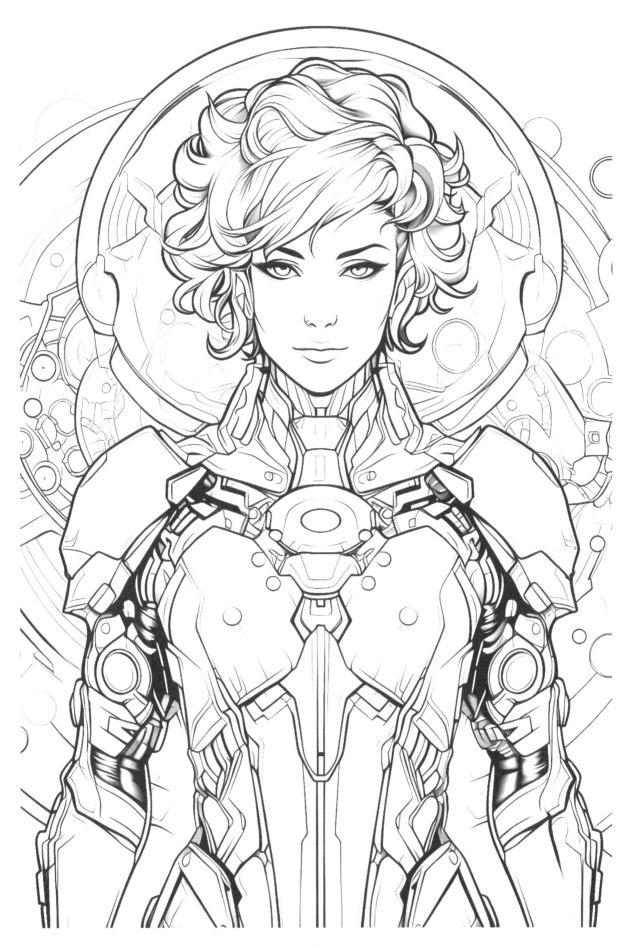

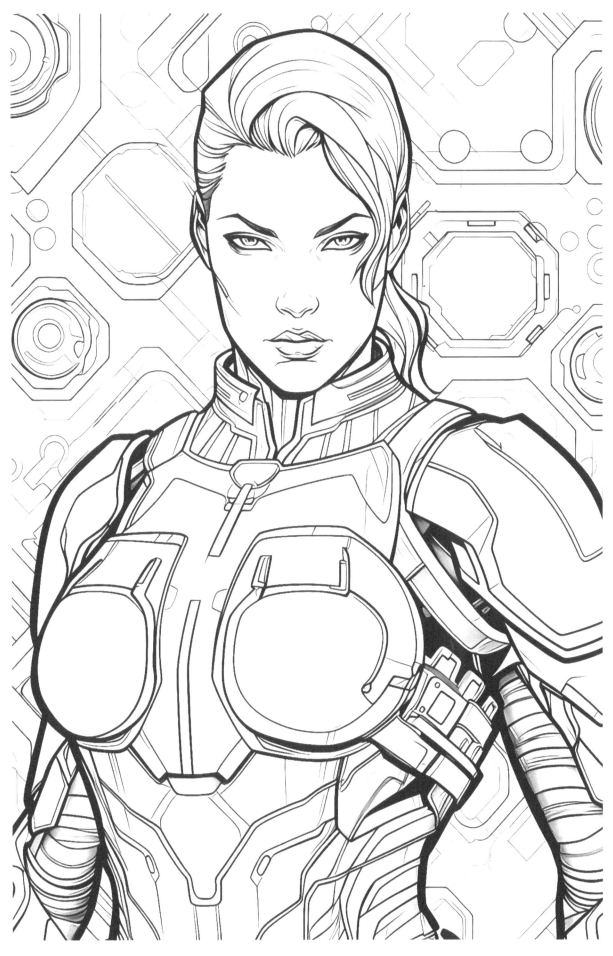

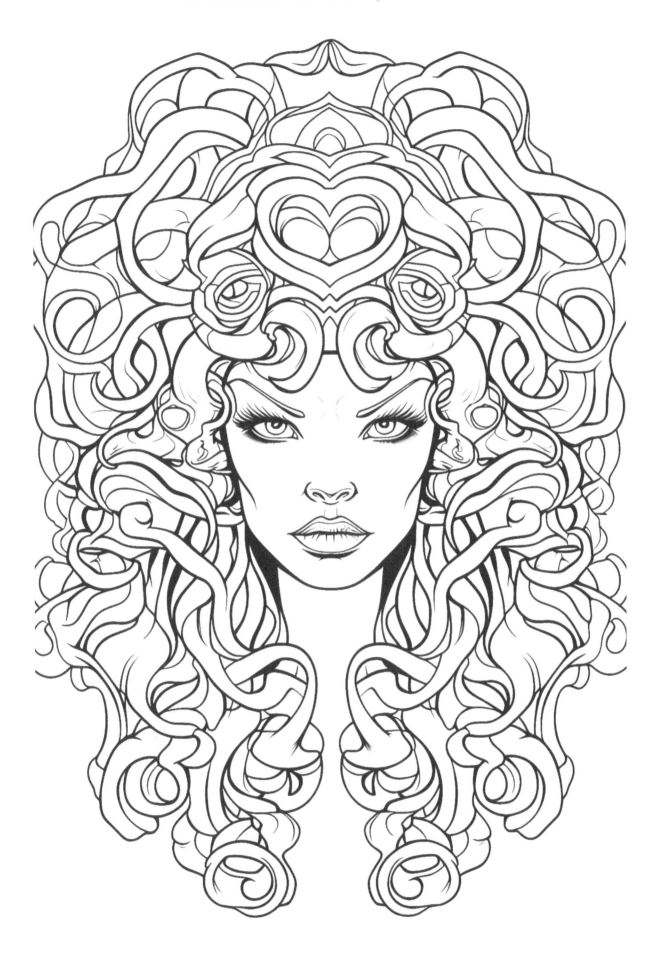

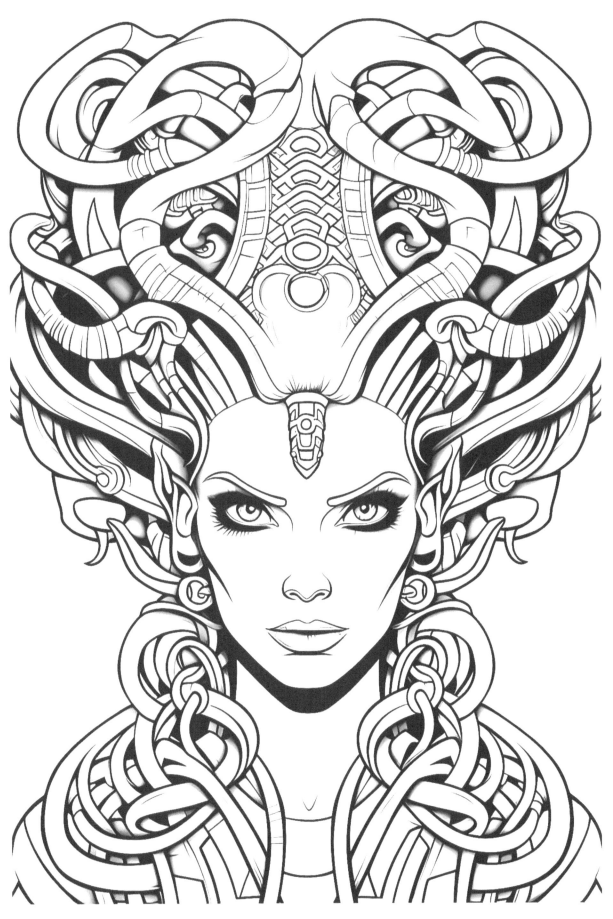

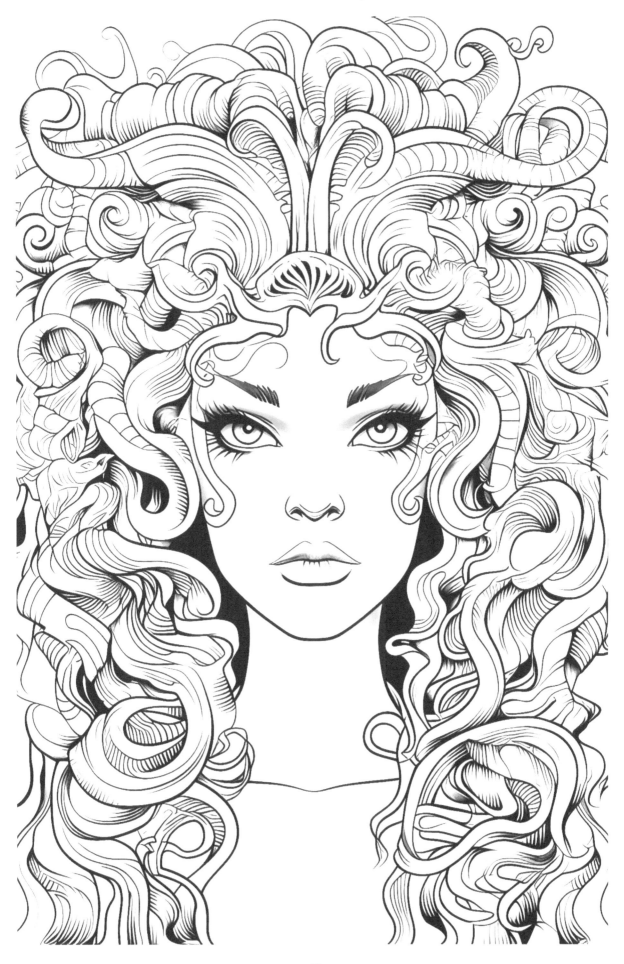

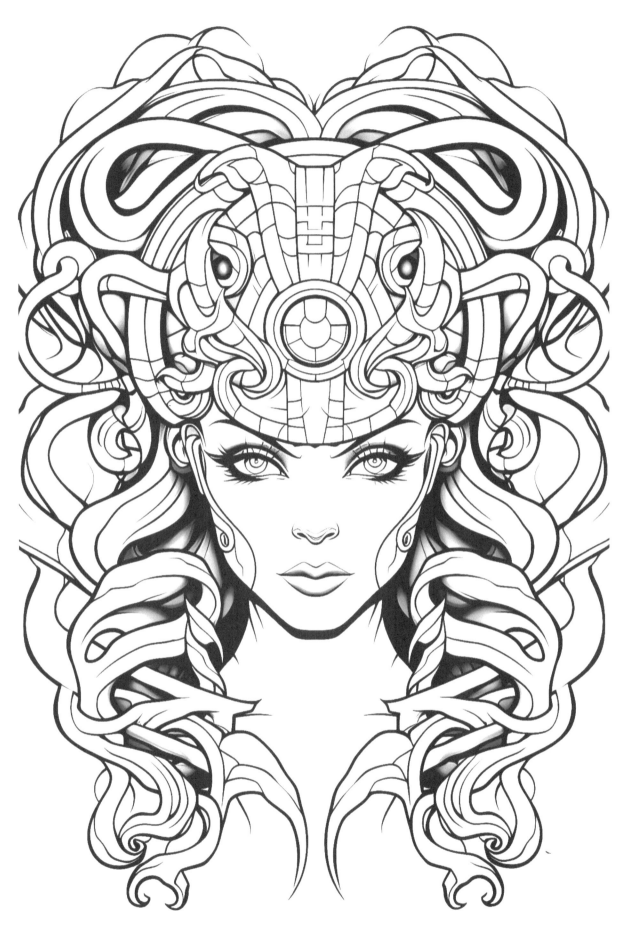

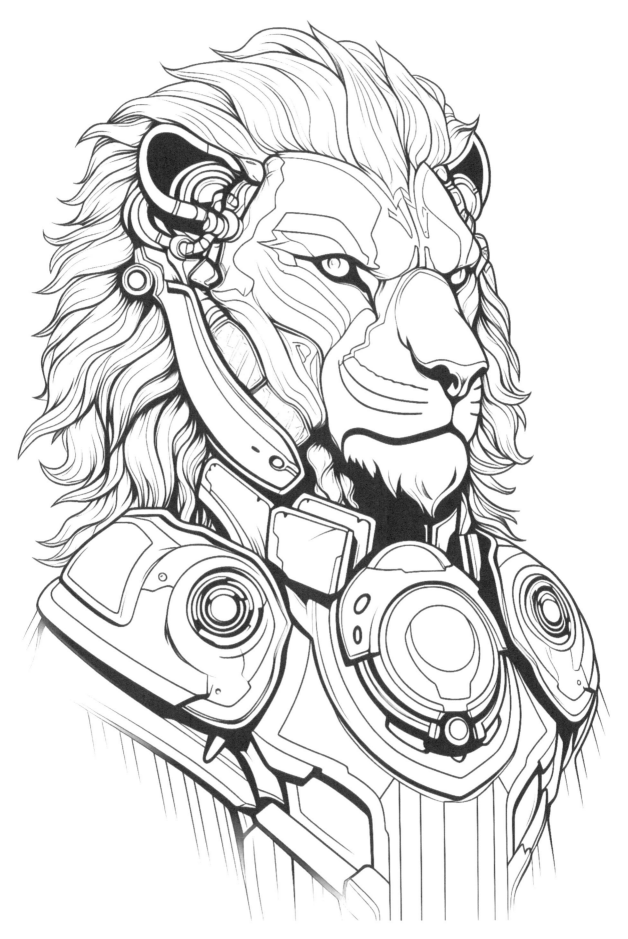

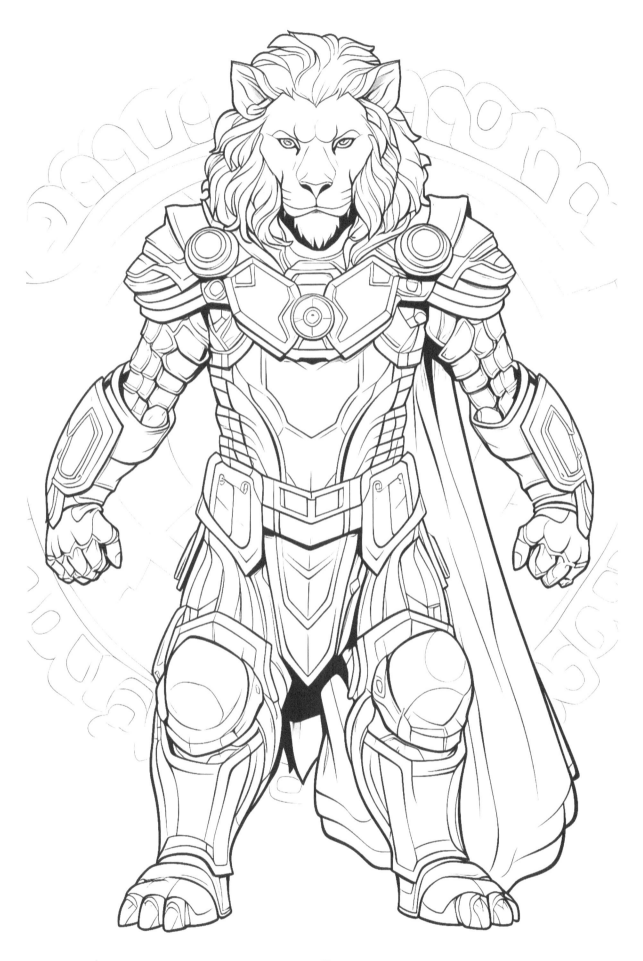

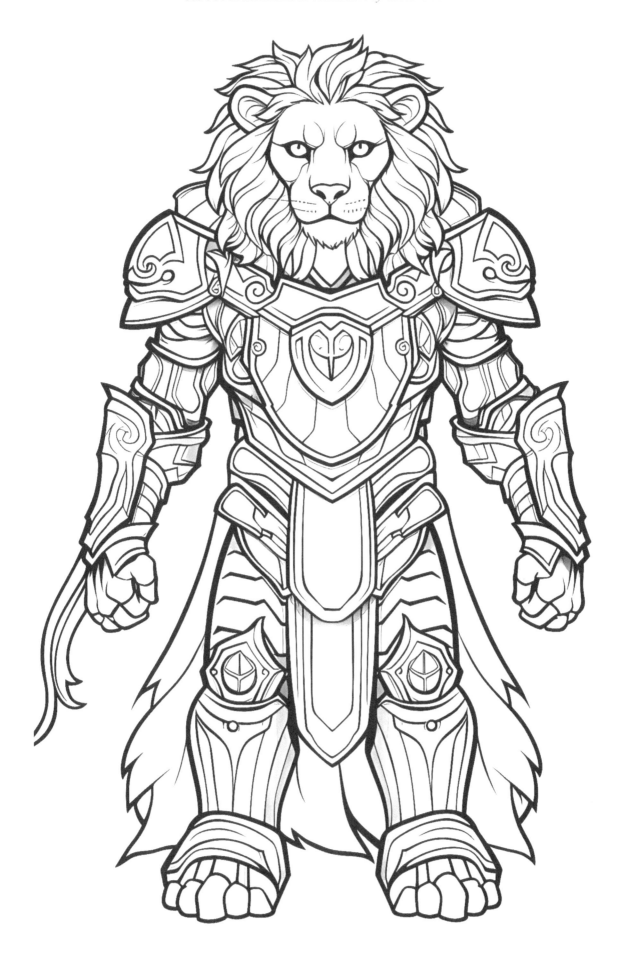

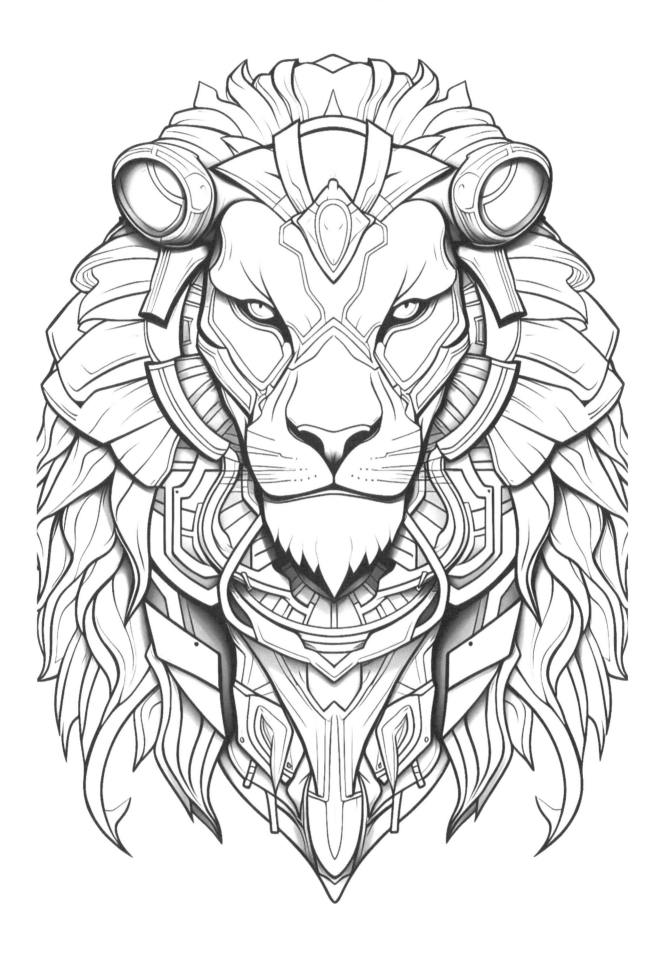

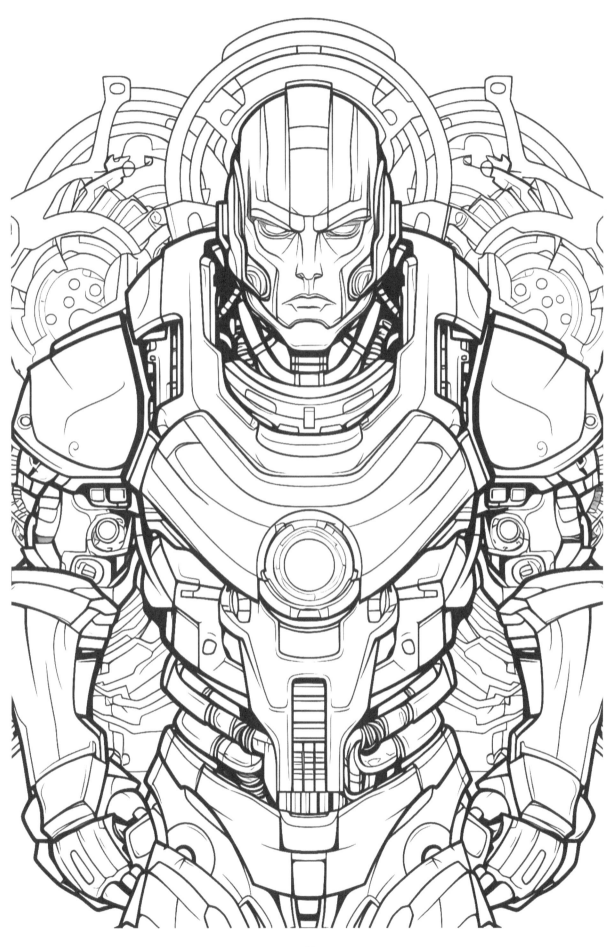

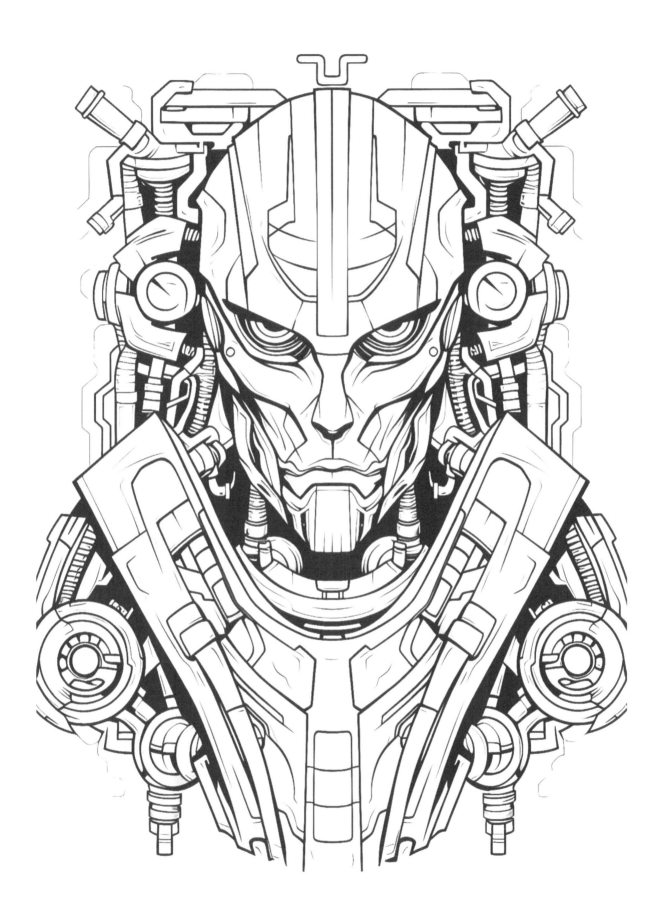

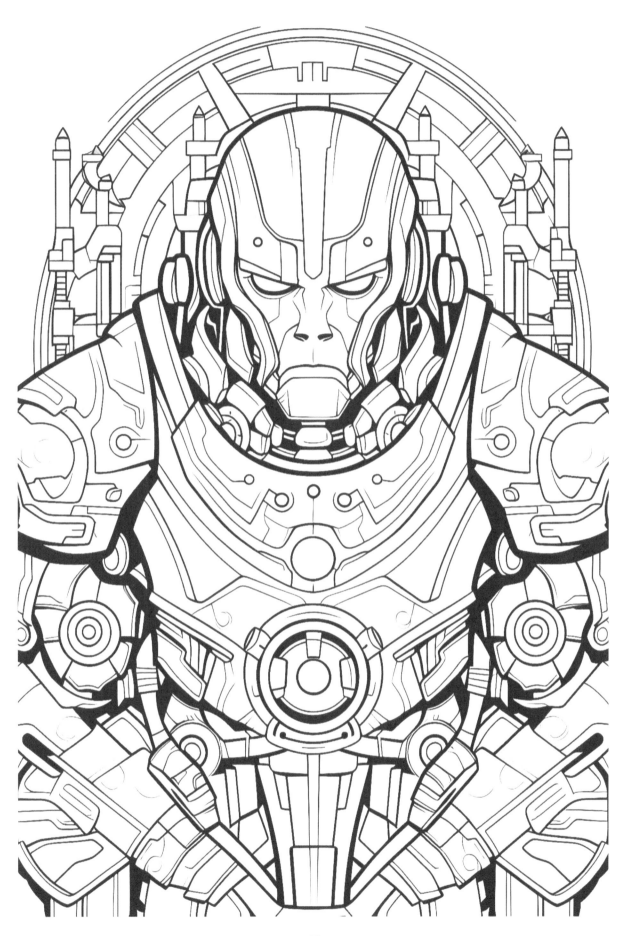

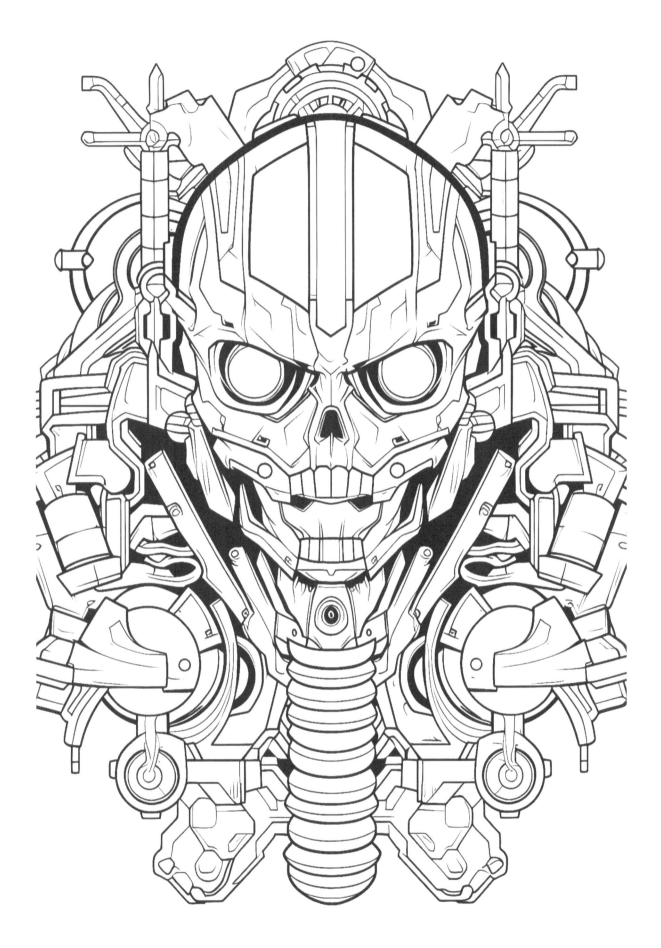

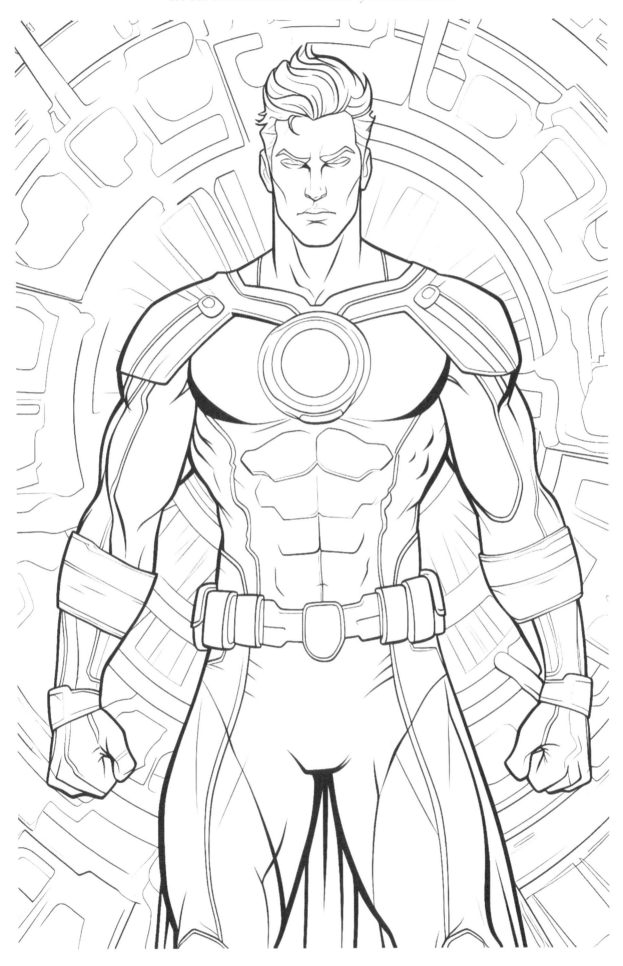

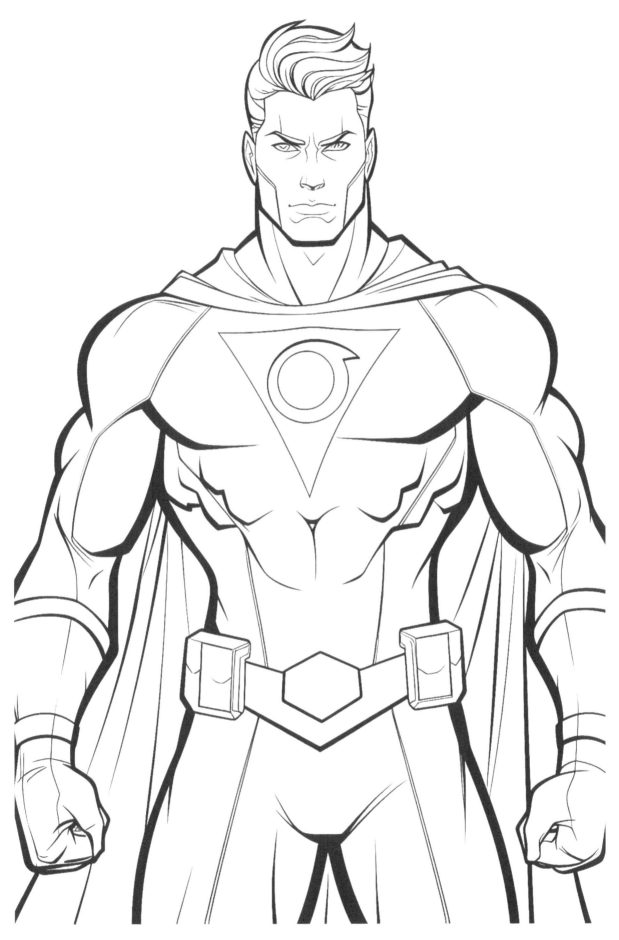

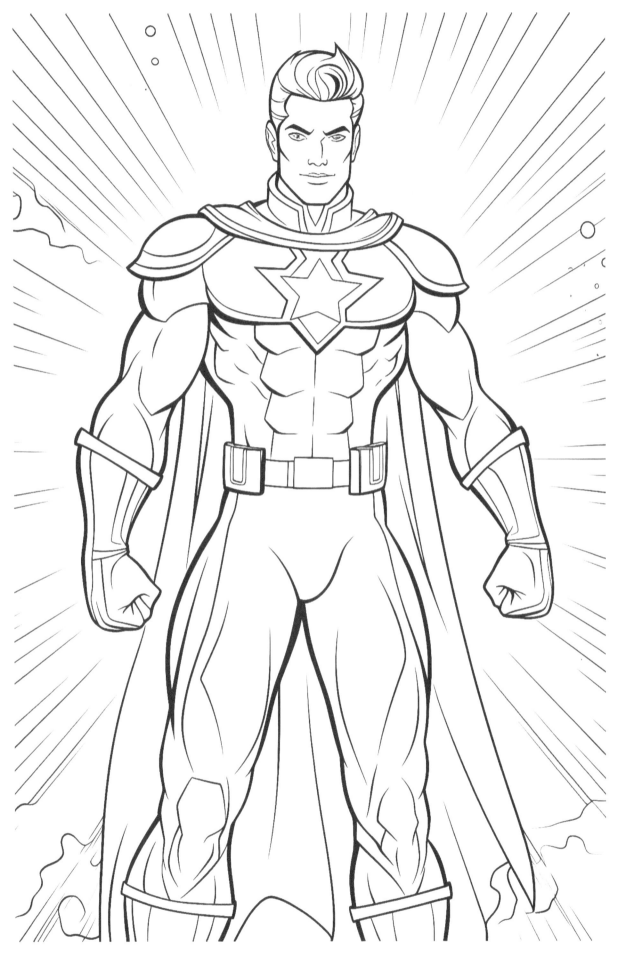

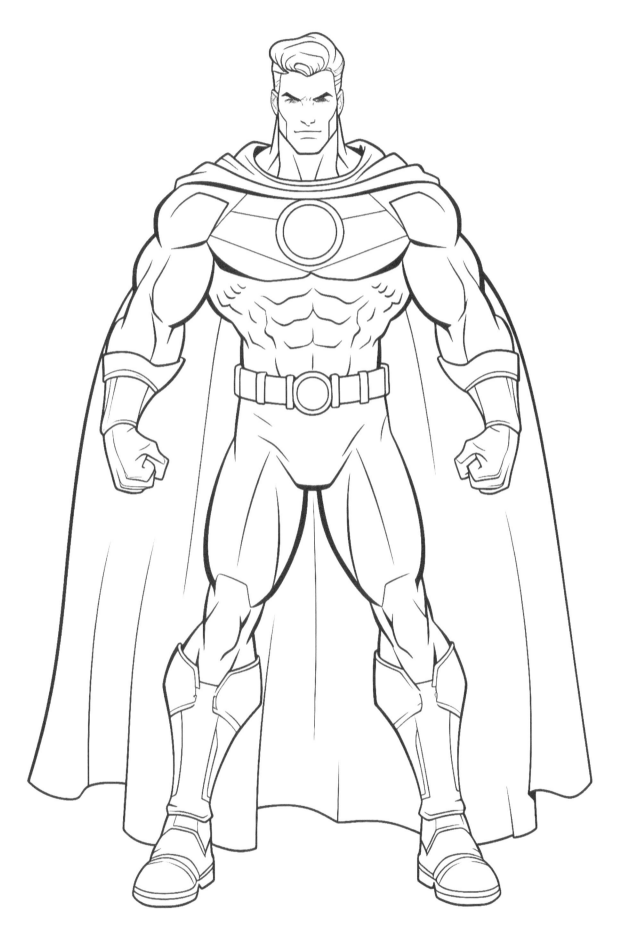

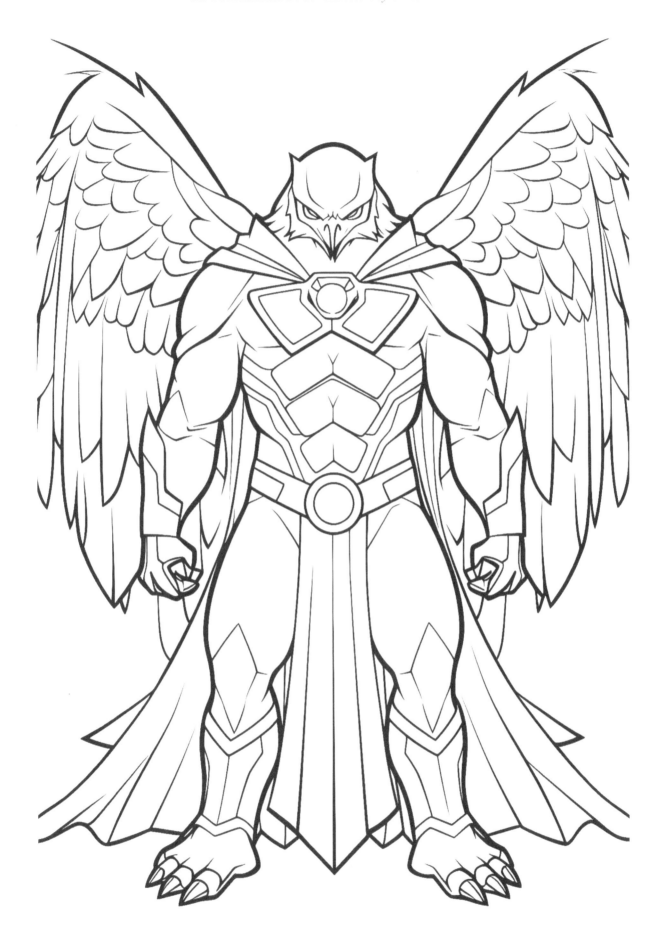

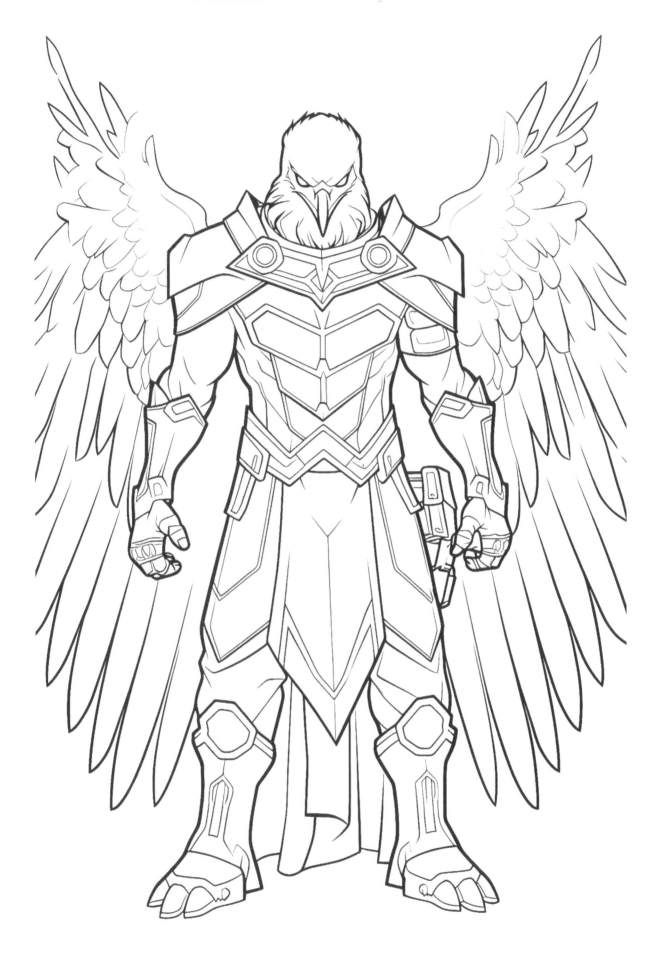

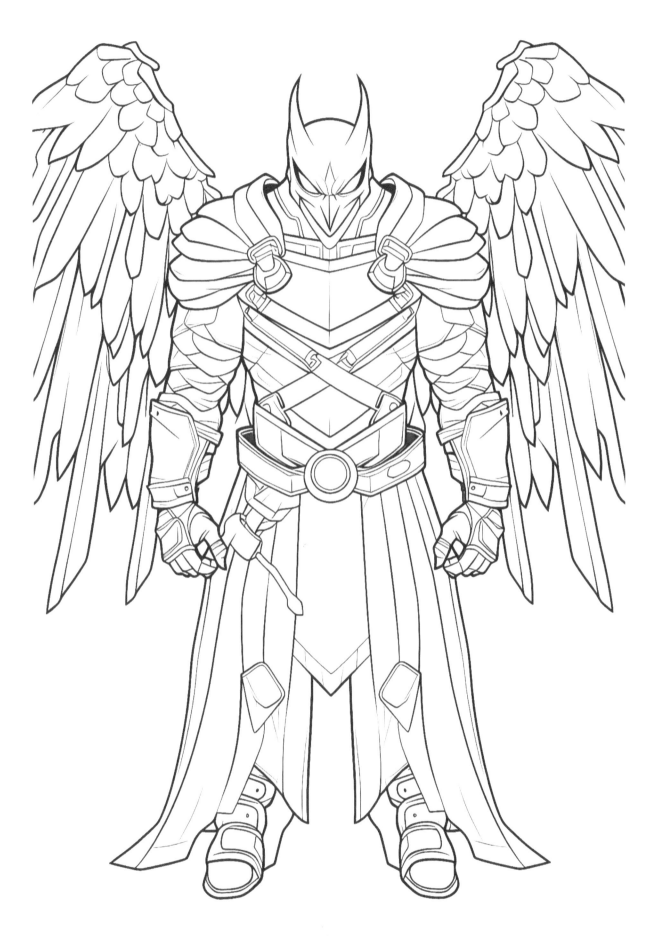

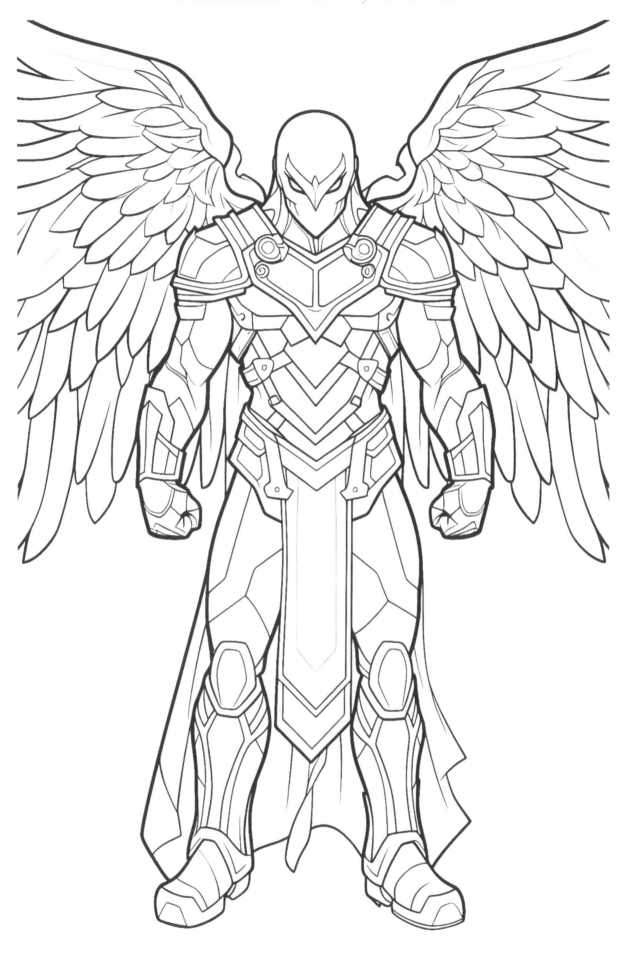

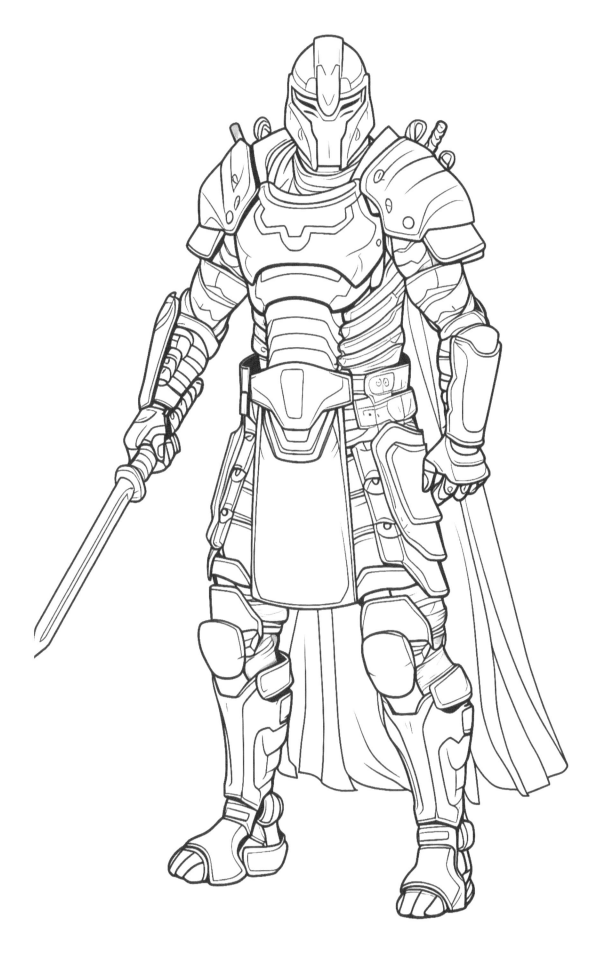

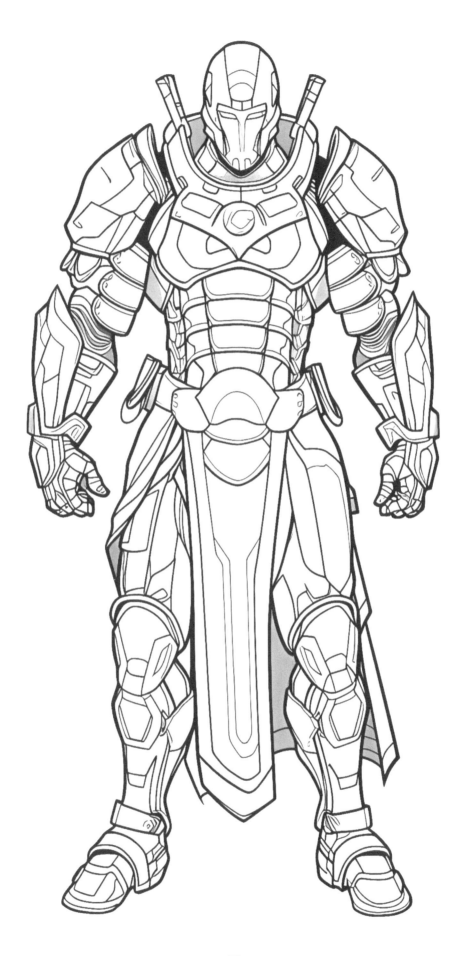

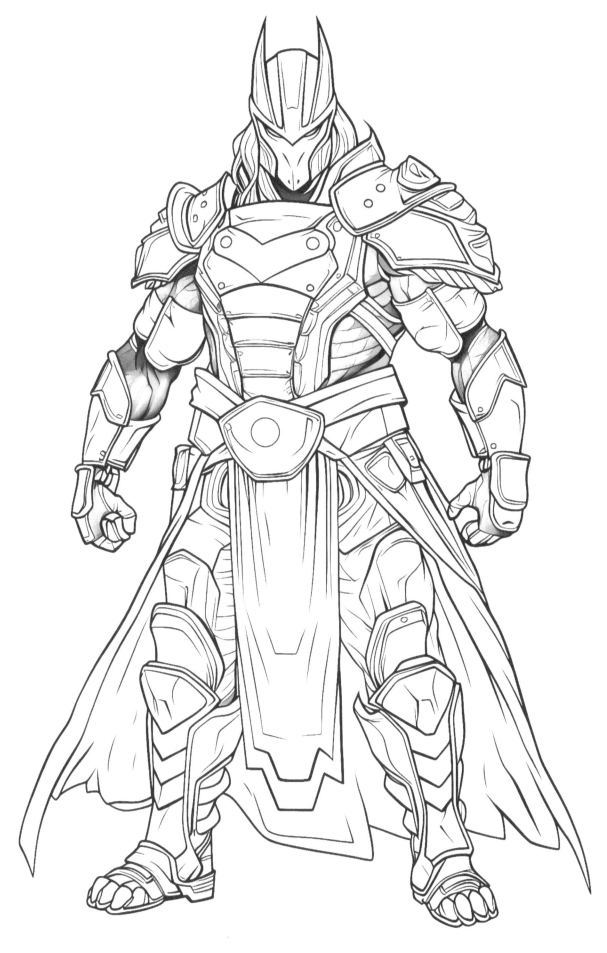

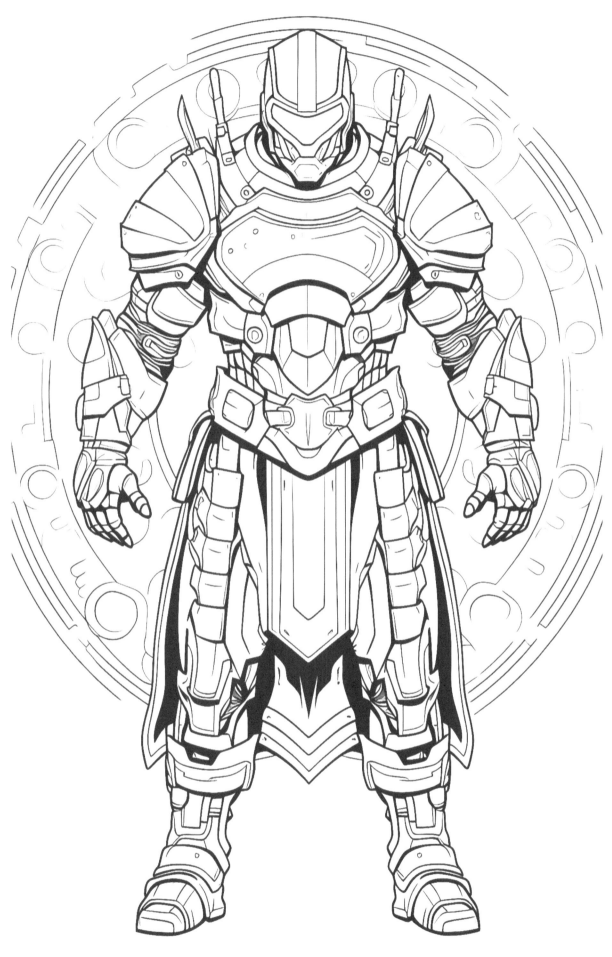

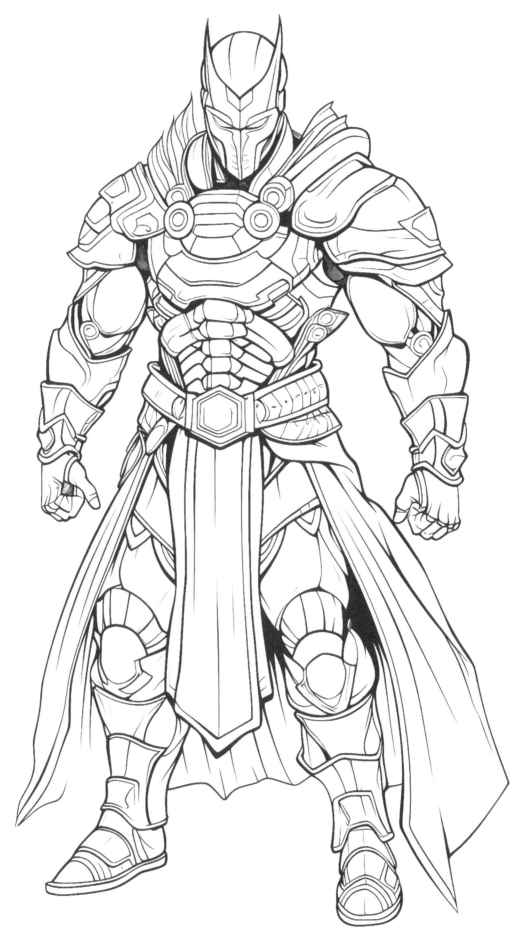

100 SUPERHEROES & VILLAINS *by* CLARA BLAKE

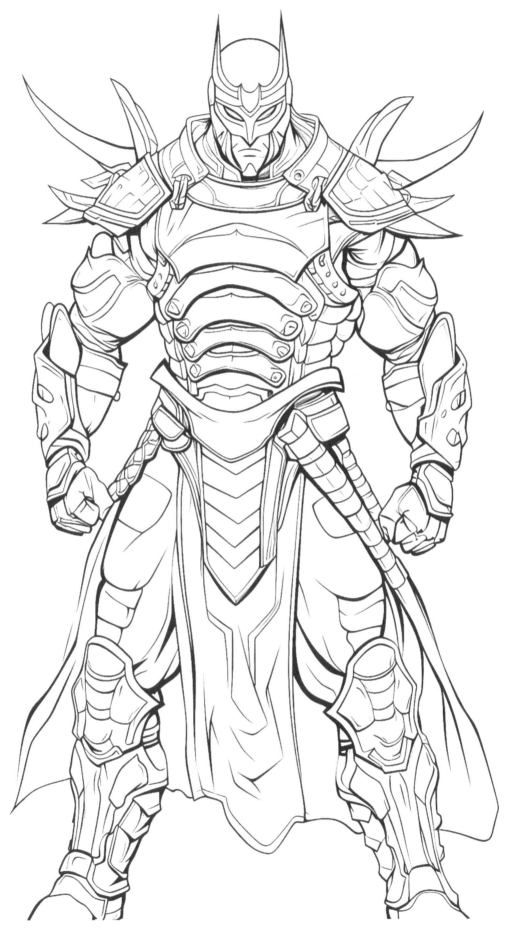

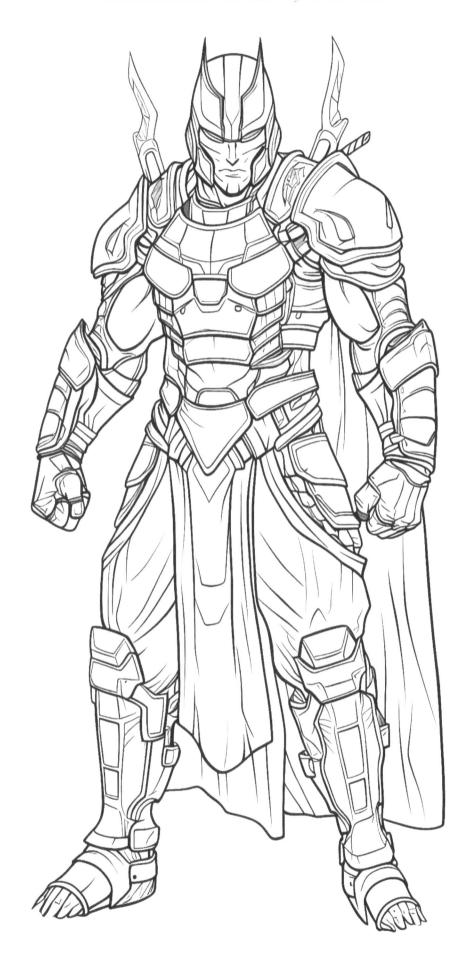

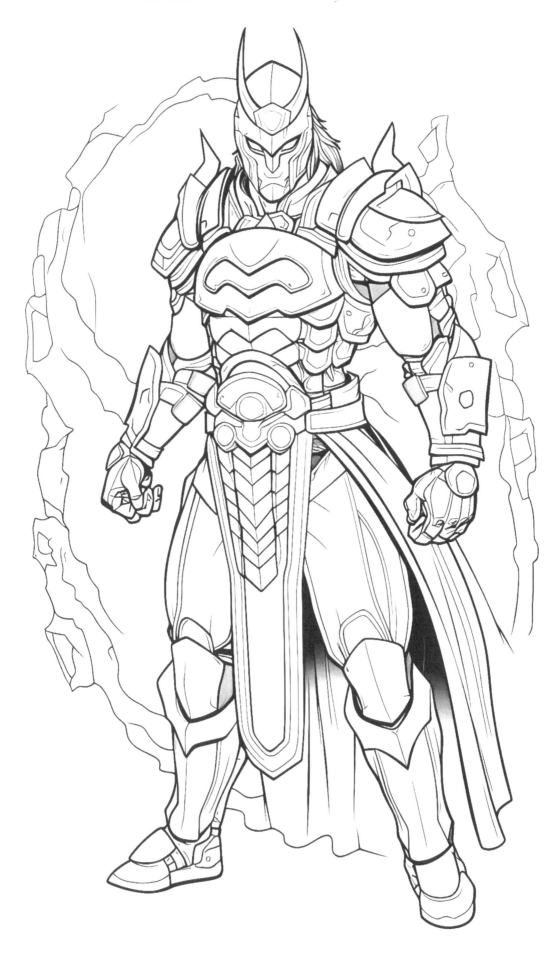

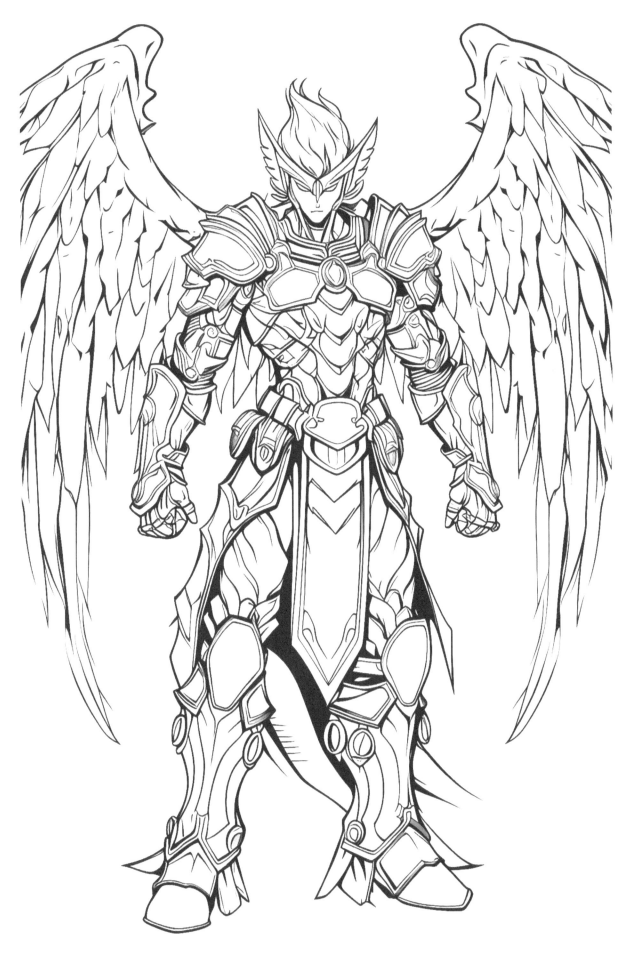

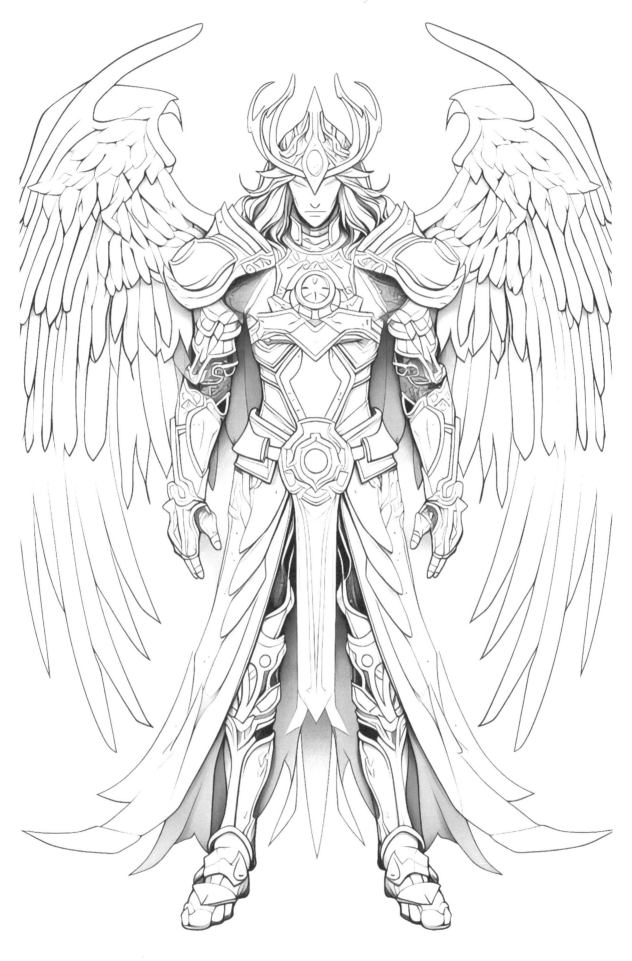

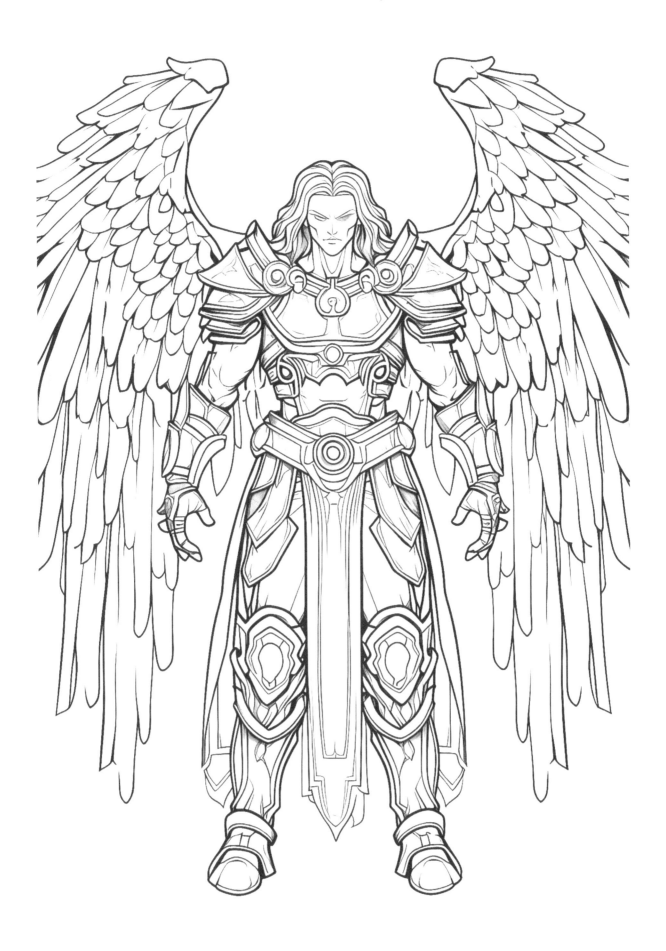

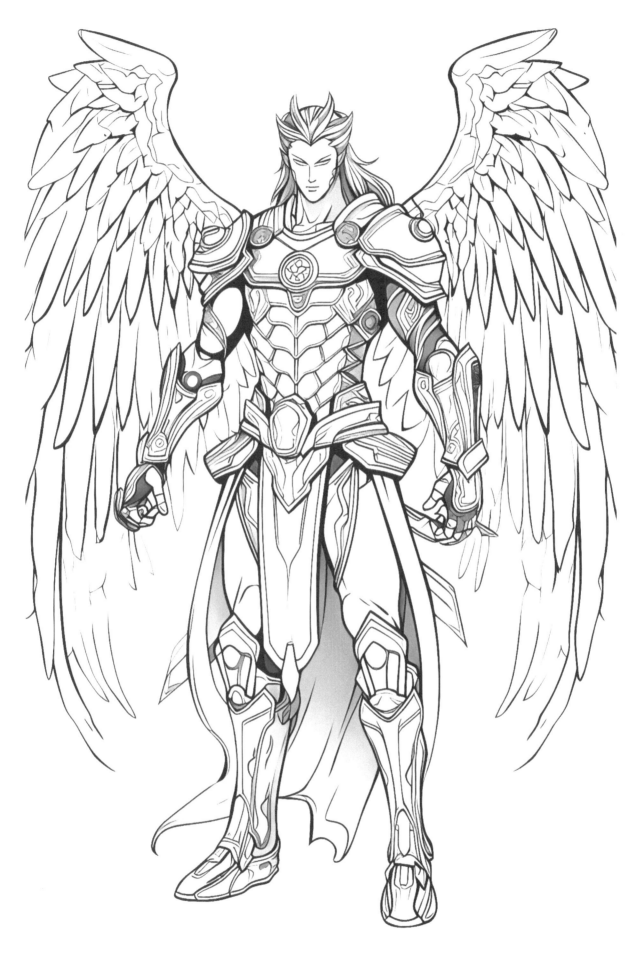

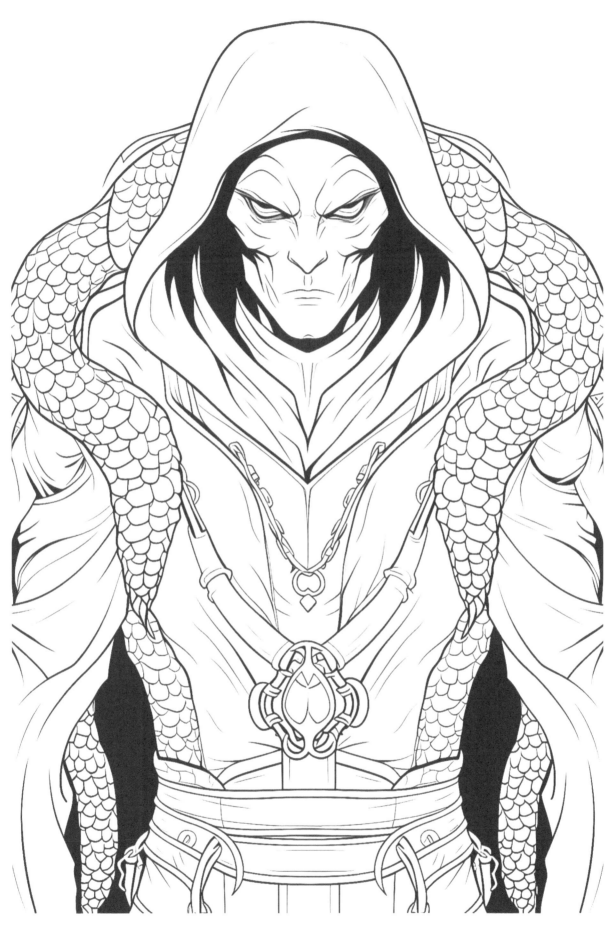

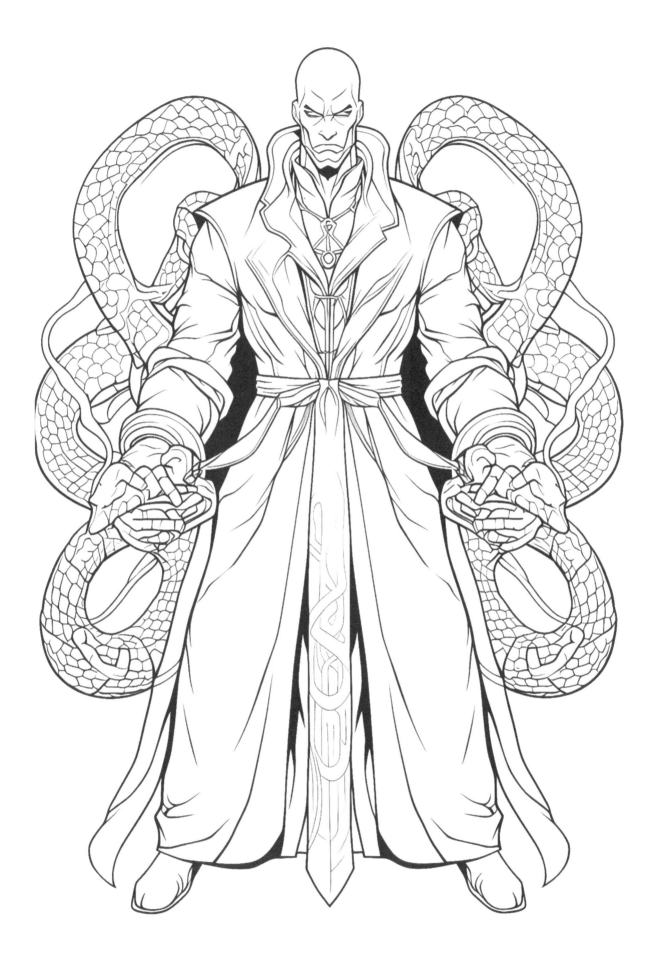

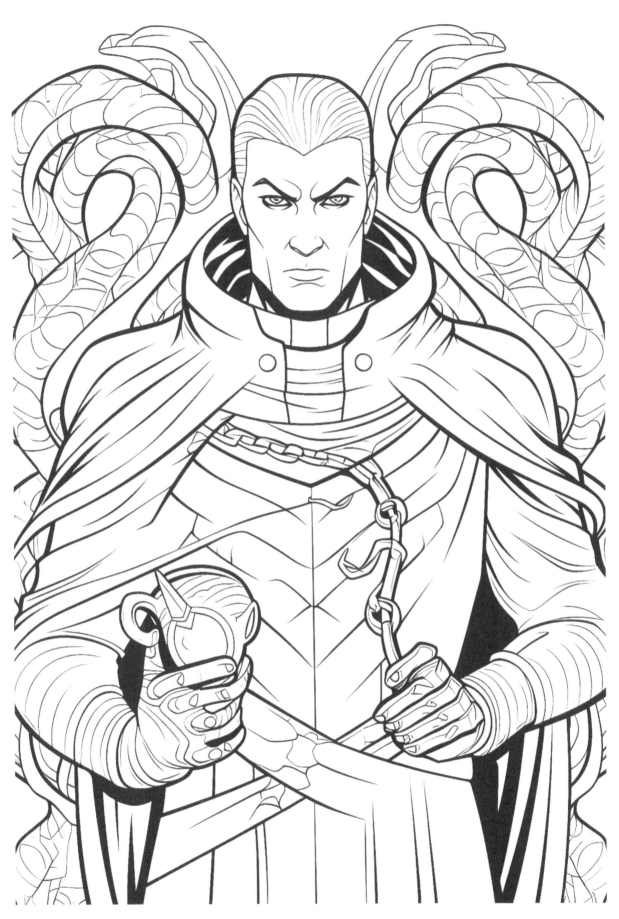

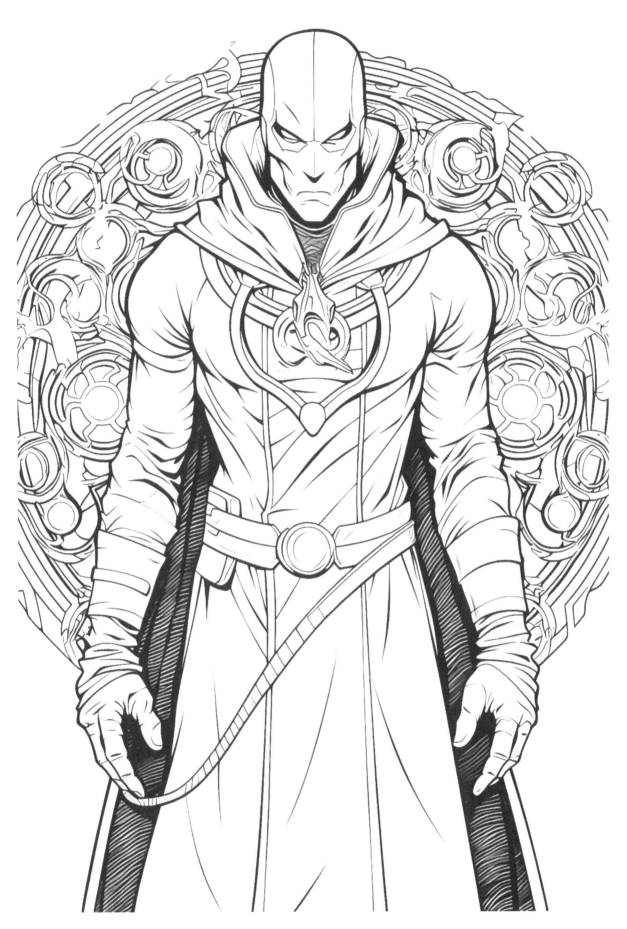

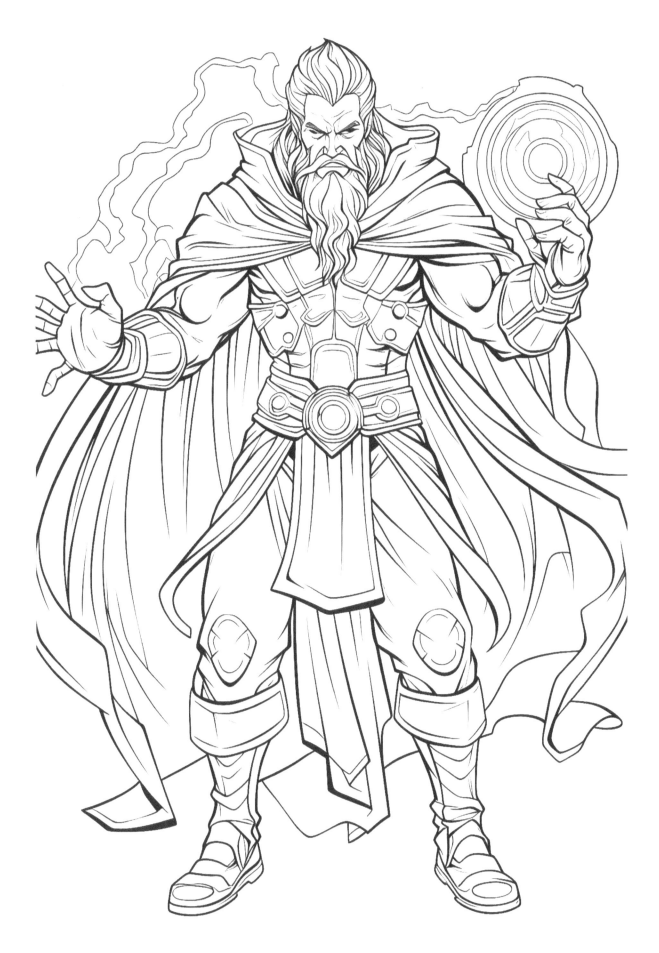

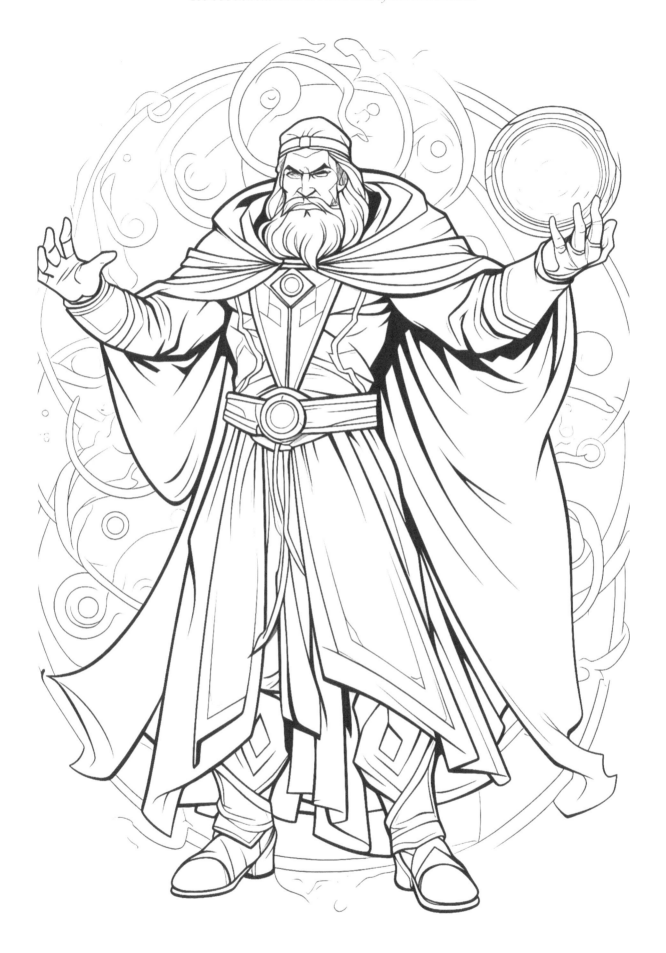

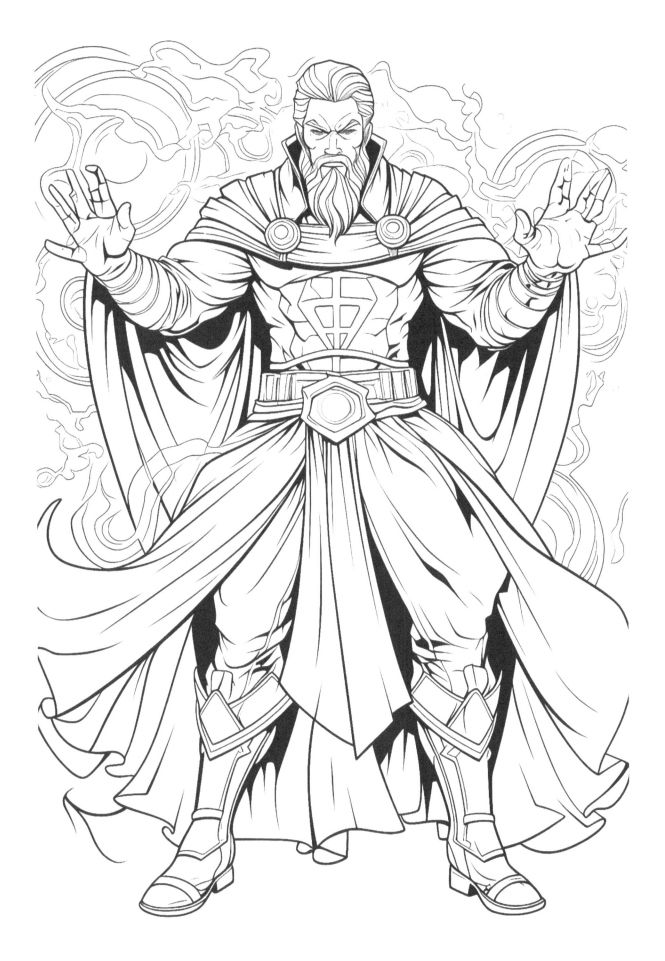

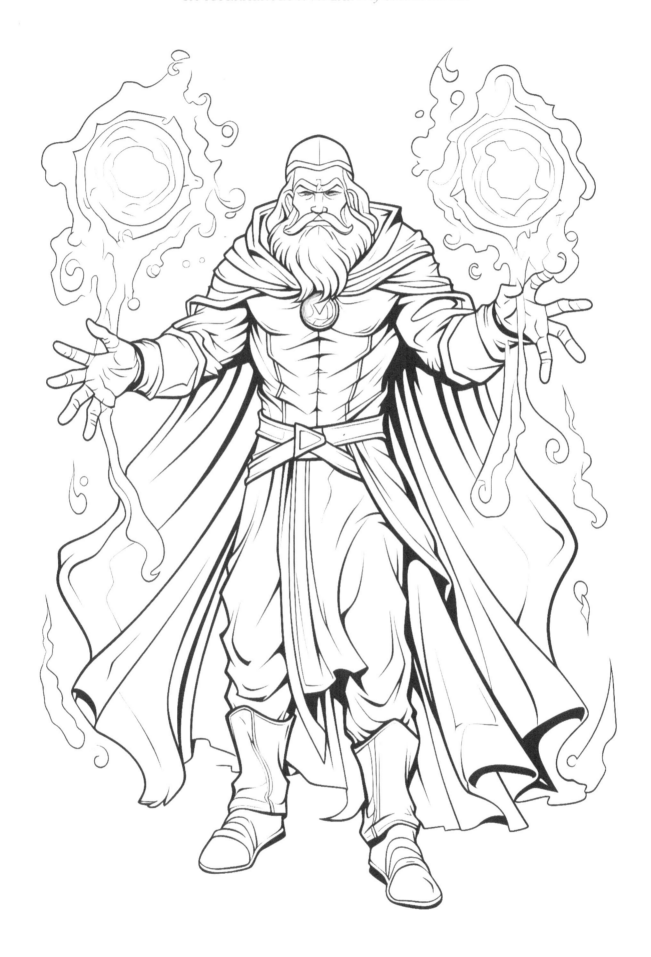

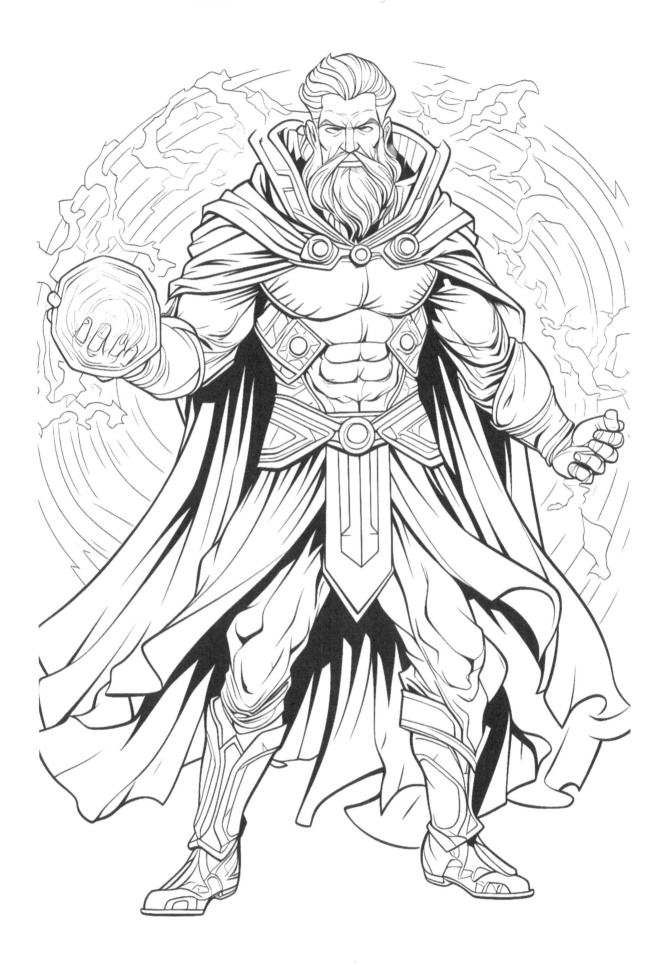

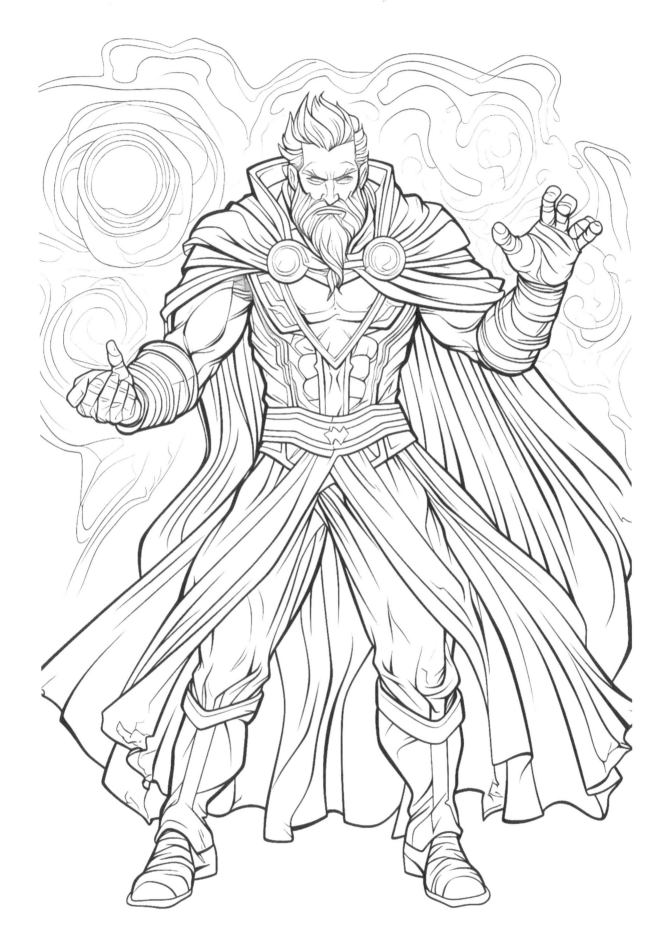

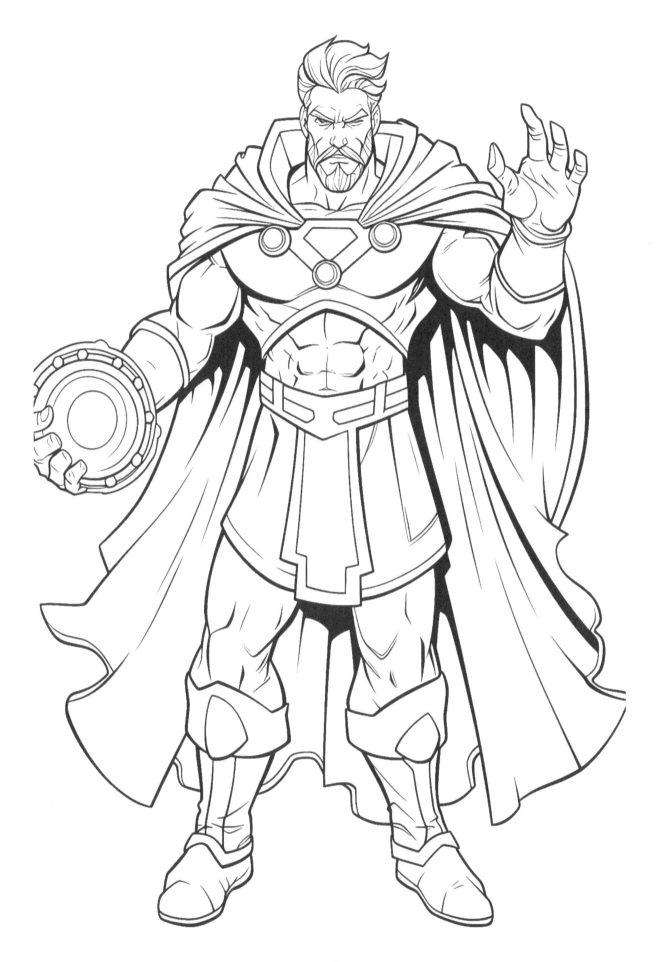

You will also love these other titles by
Clara Blake

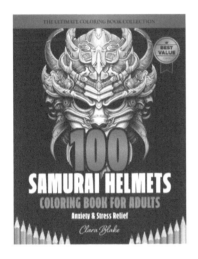
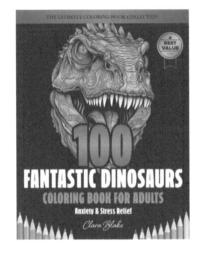
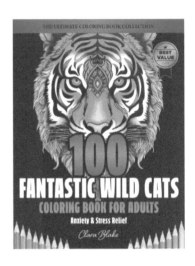
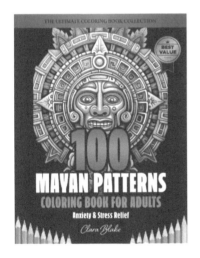
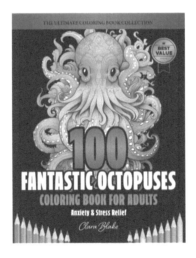
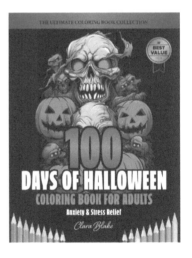

More than 100 titles available at your favorite bookstore!

Made in United States
Troutdale, OR
11/10/2024